MW00973121

Lean Forward is a Scripture-saturated reading that made me thirsty for more of God and His Truth. *Laurel Griffith writes transparently and tenderly, and brings to the pages a compelling message of spiritual transformation and the keys to keeping company with Christ.*

—**Billy Irvin**, Director of Ministry Relations, Faith Radio

Lean Forward contains powerful real life applications *that are easily translated to my own life.*

— **Walter Hill**, Chief Executive Officer, Wiregrass United Way

To reach out to God, you must first lean forward, and a good way to do this is by first memorizing Scripture. This is what Laurel Griffith suggests in this primer on attempting a faith journey. She uses her experience of relocating to another Deep South community to illustrate the principles she advocates simply and straightforwardly in this splendid roadmap to Christian living.

— **Bert Goolsby**, Author, *The Locusts of Padgett County*

This book is a labor of love. Laurel pulls stories from her own life, the lives of those around her, and the Giver of Life and weaves them together in a conversation. She focuses our thoughts and helps us re-commit to the journey of hearing from and walking with our heavenly Father. Whether you read the book from cover to cover, or read a section at a time as a devotional aid, you will realize that Laurel has been used by the Holy Spirit, who convicts and gently calls us to a life with the Lord that is more profound than one which is lived on our own.

— **Pat Fenner** small business-owner, writer, co-owner of Mom's MorningCoffee.com

When you don't know what to do...

LEAN
FORWARD

LAUREL GRIFFITH

For Jim, my husband and my friend.
Your love makes me a better person. Thank you for believing in me.

Acknowledgments

I am grateful for those who labored with me offering insight, correction, and encouragement. Bert Goolsby, Elaine Herrin Onley, Cheri Page, and Cindi Ramsey made my words clear and prevented mistakes.

A Word about the People in This Book

The people you meet in this book are real. They graciously agreed to share their stories because they believe their experiences will bring glory to God and help other people. In a few instances, I changed their names.

ISBN 978-0-9898163-0-4

Contents

1 LIVING IN-BETWEEN:
Lean Forward

*All believers, come here and listen, let me tell you what
God did for me.*

— *Psalm 66:16 (The Message)*

I graduated from the University of Alabama in 1980 with high hopes and a
reasonable plan: take off two weeks to work on a tan; land a challenging job that
paid good money; live at home for one year to stash some cash; and marry Jim
Griffith, the young medical student, who had captured my heart.

I had an engagement ring, a diploma, and a new blue suit.

The first round of resumes brought little response. At first I was selective, but as
time went by, I lowered my expectations. I went on crazy interviews and chased
down obscure leads. My confidence plummeted. My friends went to work, and I
wondered what was wrong with me.

I prayed for opportunity and open doors. For six months I hit dead ends at every
turn. I felt terrible.

I fussed and fumed to anyone who would listen. I focused on changing my
situation and never once considered how waiting might benefit me in the future.

I never wondered if there was something I could learn or experience while I searched and prayed.

Sooner or later we all end up waiting on something: a job, a better job, a marriage partner, a better marriage, a miracle, a baby, a friend, a nicer place to live.

Waiting isn't easy. At different times in my life, I have felt as though I was treading water or running in place. I have felt trapped, stuck, and frustrated, but when I look back, I recognize God had a plan for the waiting days. The struggle has been good for me.

The purpose of this book is to share what I have learned from the seasons of in-between.

Waiting isn't supposed to be a passive, twiddling-thumbs kind of experience. When we wait on God, we focus our attention. We position ourselves to hear Him speak.

The prophet describes it this way. "Since ancient times no one has heard, no ear has perceived, no eye has seen any God besides you, who acts on behalf of those who wait for him. You come to the help of those who gladly do right, who remember your ways" (Isa. 64: 4–5a).

God loves us perfectly. He has promised to work in our lives and circumstances when we are ready and the time is right. To grasp God's guidance, there are obstacles I must eliminate. To receive God's instruction, there are practices I should embrace.

I have discovered our Heavenly Father speaks during every season of life, but sometimes I miss the message.

When I was twenty-three years old, I was too busy complaining to consider there might be a reason for what was happening or wasn't happening in my life. I didn't know waiting could make me a better person.

There were days I wanted to take control. I felt like Abram, who got so tired of waiting on the Lord, he slept with Hagar to produce an heir.

Sometimes I felt like the Israelites wandering in the wilderness. I knew there was a Promised Land, but for the life of me, I could not see it on the horizon. Some days I cried out like Hannah and wondered if God was really listening. *Could He hear me? Did He care?*

One evening in October, six months after graduation, I received a phone call from someone I had never met. He claimed to represent a company from another state. He wanted to interview me for a public relations position. The man said he found my resume on file with a local professional organization.

Skeptical but desperate, I agreed to meet the recruiter at the Holiday Inn. He said the new office was under construction. Jim went with me and sat in the car just in case the potential job was really a scam.

As it turned out, the guy was legitimate and so was the company. Expanding to the Birmingham region, the organization needed all kinds of help. Grateful and excited, I accepted the offer.

In the following weeks, my new position taught me a great deal about business. Since the company was a start up, I received more responsibility than I would have had at an established firm. The fast-paced environment taught me to work hard and think on my feet.

Dewey Crim, the president of the Birmingham operation, loved and followed Jesus. He led our organization with integrity and treated me like a daughter. The week before Jim and I married, my co-workers presented me with a generous check as a wedding gift. The company offered me a promotion and a raise.

I look back on all the jobs I thought I wanted and realize this opportunity turned out to be far better than anything I could have imagined. God answered my prayer at the perfect time, with the perfect gift.

My only regret is how I how I spent the days of in-between.

Three months after I started work, physicians diagnosed my mother with a brain tumor. She faced immediate surgery and subsequent radiation and chemotherapy. Although we had some good days, she declined rapidly. Everything about our lives changed.

The in-between days I lived in my parents' home were the last good times I had with my mom. If I had known the future, I would not have been so distracted and concerned about me. But God, who sees the end from the beginning, knew what was to come. He gave me a gift I did not know I needed. Today, I look back in gratitude for the time I tried to wish away.

This book is neither a formula nor a set of religious rules. Your belief is not in yourself and what you do but in God's provision and care. Each chapter describes a way to prepare your heart and your mind to hear the voice of God. The actions described in these pages allow you to open yourself to the Spirit. It is always God who does the teaching and the guiding.

To receive the truth we need, we must decide to cooperate with the Spirit of God. We must desire the transformation of the heart that only a connection with God will bring. We begin by positioning ourselves to hear from God. The process reminds me of my first day on skis.

After a bunny slope tutorial, I headed for the lift. My heart pounded while my young husband and I stood in line, waiting on the chair to scoop us up and take us to the top of the run. Anxious about my exit, I didn't even notice the breathtaking scenery.

The couple in front of us made everything seem so easy. When it became our turn, Jim skied off and glanced over his shoulder. He could not have seen me at first because I wasn't on the slope at all. I sat frozen—stuck like glue to my seat. The attendant screamed at me. Then he grudgingly stopped the lift and walked my chair back up the mountain so this southern girl could scramble off in shame.

I half skied and half scooted down the snowy trail, intending to turn in my rented equipment and head for the coffee shop. Jim persuaded me to try again.

"You'll do it this time," he encouraged as we glided upwards. We were getting close, and I felt jittery. What if the attendant had to rescue me a second time? I would be kicked off the mountain or relegated to the rope tow for the rest of our vacation.

"Get ready," Jim ordered as he grabbed my hand.

"Lean forward. Lean forward. Lean forward! Now, go!"

The phrase that got me off the chair lift became a family joke and ultimately a way of thinking about my relationship with God.

When I cling to the safe and familiar, I miss opportunities to learn and grow. It's impossible for me to grab hold of God's plan for my future when I'm determined to stay where I am.

Are you facing an obstacle or struggling for direction? Are you waiting for an open door?

I don't know your situation or the answer to your problem, but I know the One who does. God isn't holding out on you. You don't have to jump through hoops to get to the information you need. You don't have to check a few boxes to make it to His loving arms.

God cares. God speaks. God gives. He has the truth you need and the path for you to follow. Focus your thoughts. Prepare your heart. *Get ready to hear from God.*

2 LEAN FORWARD:
Memorize Scripture

Years ago I memorized Scripture to get cool stuff.

My Sunday School teacher recorded our names on scrapbook-worthy certificates. Colored stickers indicated the extent of our commitment—red for showing up, blue for sporadic results, and a large gold seal reserved for the few who memorized each week's verses. In the fifth grade the competition grew more intense. A flashy golden charm bracelet was the much-coveted girl "prize". We knew the Ten Commandments; I didn't say we obeyed them.

Eventually my friends and I achieved the pinnacle of Scripture memorization. *We were crowned with real tiaras, standing in front of the entire church.*

By the time I entered high school, I had platform shoes, a macramé belt, and a decade of Bible verses hidden in my heart and on the tip of my tongue. Unfortunately from that point forward, my commitment to memory work dwindled. Through the years, I taught Bible classes and relished study—even digging down deep into commentaries and challenging books. I kept prayer journals and spent time daily with God. I published a Christian magazine that encouraged people to memorize Scripture. While thankful for the verses learned in childhood, I struggled as an adult. My Bible verse memorization became haphazard, guilt-driven and often felt like a chore rather than a privilege. I lacked the passion, and so I did not do the work.

But in the summer of 2010, my husband and I moved to the country. There, God used His Word to change my life.

Our family home sold unexpectedly, and we found ourselves scrambling for a place to live. Jim's friend and colleague offered to rent us his beloved farmhouse, a unique and charming place with a fishing pond Jim liked. I'm not a country girl, but I thought a few months on the farm might feel like a vacation.

After we had unpacked most of the boxes, I mentioned to Jim that I needed to join a gym since there was no place for my treadmill. He said something that made me laugh out loud. "Laurel, would you enjoy getting your exercise right here on the farm?"

Was he kidding? I couldn't imagine spending so much time alone in a pasture, but Jim seemed determined to mow a trail around the perimeter of the fields. My husband sounded downright eager to drive the big tractor, so I tried to remain positive.

Early Monday morning I stepped outside to investigate the new path. As I walked, I began to talk to God out loud. The cows appeared unfazed as though they saw this kind of behavior all the time.

A few days later, a pretty white kitten appeared on our back step. Jim reminded me we weren't cat people, but I was sure he had forgotten about the recent "mouse-in-the-pantry episode." I thought Dovey the cat could certainly earn her keep. With great surprise I discovered the "she" was really a "he." As I explained to our kids when they came home for Thanksgiving, anyone would have come to the same conclusion. After all, he arrived with a little pink collar. The vet corrected my mistake, but the name stuck. For the record, the cat didn't seem to mind.

The four of us—two crazy, barking dogs, one woman in an Indiana Jones hat (Alabama sun), carrying a big walking stick (Alabama snakes), and the kitten— left the house every morning for our three-mile walk. The dogs ran ahead, circled back, and ran ahead again. Dovey kept up as long as he could, and when he tuckered out, I carried him until he caught his breath. Some days, army helicopters flew overhead, their engines punctuating our peace. (The farm sat below a flight-training path, and the landing strip lay only a mile or so away.) At one point I realized that as the noise grew louder, I raised my voice too—as if I needed to make sure God could still hear me over the roar. I describe the spectacle only because one should understand this was not some pious, picture-perfect event, but a quirky mix of animals, pilot-training, exercise, and God.

I had been walking and praying for a few weeks when our adult Sunday School class received a challenge. A new member encouraged us to memorize Scripture. He said we should begin with a verse or two each week. He told us how God used Scripture memory in his life. He agreed to lead us and hold us accountable. Since we didn't know him very well, it seemed impolite to say no.

The first week I wrote the verses on an index card and carried them with me while I walked. Sometimes I repeated the verse aloud; sometimes I prayed. Amazingly, at the end of the week I had successfully committed Psalm 1 to memory. I would say a verse and then ask God to help me be the person who would avoid temptation, delight in his Word, and bear fruit in season.

The next Sunday morning, the new guy gave us another memory assignment. And so the pattern began. I repeated the same phrase, sometimes dozens of times, until it lodged in my brain. Then I added the next sentence. Some days I would memorize an entire verse, while on other days I would remember just a portion. I didn't worry about how much I was accomplishing. Scripture memory added depth and richness to my praying and walking routine. The Spirit stirred my soul.

The process moved me to a deeper experience with God. I repeated the verses, talked to God about them, and asked Him to show me how the passage related to my life.

"Blessed is the one who does not walk in step with the wicked or stand in the way that sinners take or sit in the company of mockers, but whose delight is in the law of the Lord, and who meditates on his law day and night. That person is like a tree planted by streams of water, which yields its fruit in season and whose leaf does not wither—whatever they do prospers" (Ps. 1:1-3).

The more I memorized and prayed, the more excited I became about what God was doing. When my mind would have normally shifted to neutral, I found myself repeating Scripture in my head. Sometimes I made a conscious decision to review a passage I was learning, while at other times I repeated it unintentionally. Verses drifted in my mind as I went to sleep. Scripture would be my first thought when I opened my eyes the next morning.

Much confusion exists about meditation in the Christian community. Many believers run from the practice because it sounds like it belongs in a new-age cult or Far-Eastern religion. Some of us avoid meditation because it feels difficult and strained. If we have been Christians for a while, we know what Bible reading and prayer look like, but because meditation is done privately, we don't have any examples to follow. We don't know what to do or how to do it, and we aren't really sure we want to meditate at all.

Richard Foster describes what happens when we begin to meditate. "The perpetual presence of the Lord (omnipresence, as we say) moves from a theological dogma to a radiant reality."[1]

No longer are we talking about God; rather, we begin to experience His very presence. The routine of life becomes a place where we encounter God because His Words constantly run through our minds—even when we shop for groceries, correct an employee, or wait in traffic.

At some point I stumbled into meditation. It felt like an accident on my part, but I think God planned for this to happen all along.

Day after day, God spoke to me in a way I had never previously experienced. I inhaled, consumed, existed off the very Word of God. I craved more and added verses to my memory book. (By now, I carried a spiral book of note cards so I could simply flip from page to page as I walked.)

Walking and quoting verses became an expression of true worship, as I found myself proclaiming with the psalmist: "Praise the Lord, my soul; all my inmost being, praise his holy name." [2]

I stood on the top of the hill, lifted my arms to heaven and met God in that place. *I praise you, God. You are holy and all-knowing. You are all-powerful. You are filled with love. You are Creator, Redeemer, Counselor, and Friend. You have my life and everything in this world is in your control. I love you, Lord!*

"Praise the Lord, my soul, and forget not all his benefits" —
Thank you for Jim and the kids, our health, our freedom, the material blessings you have provided. Thank you for our church and for our friends. You have given us so many good things.

" . . . who forgives all your sins"
Please show me my sin. I want to know the places in my heart where I am holding on to envy or pride or anything else that might keep me from seeing you. Please forgive the unkind words I spoke today.

" . . . and heals all your diseases,"
I ask you to help Daddy feel better. Guide his doctors and show them what to do. I pray that the medicine will work.

" . . . who redeems your life from the pit and crowns you with love and compassion."
I worshipped the God who paid for my sin on the cross and who lifted me from the depth of many pits—depression and fear to name a couple—and who continued to pour His love over me in such lavish ways.

" . . . who satisfies your desires with good things so that your youth is renewed like the eagle's."
I thanked Him for meaningful work. I thanked Him for the richness of our lives. I felt alive and energized because God had awakened me to His presence.

Some days I walked and repeated verses, and I begged God to work in a friend's life: "Blessed are those who hunger and thirst for righteousness, for they will be filled" (Matt. 5:6).
They are in a mess Lord, and you are the only answer. Help them to see it. Help them to desire you more than anything else.

Some days I asked for direction: "Trust in the Lord with all your heart, and lean not on your own understanding; in all your ways submit to him, and he will direct your paths" (Prov. 3:5–6).
God, I don't know what to do now. Please guide me through this confusion.

In November, Jim gave me a pair of ugly boots for my birthday. Even though they made my feet look like concrete blocks, they kept me warm and dry during the winter months. I continued to meet God on the farm trail, engaging in worship, prayer, memory, and meditation as I reviewed verses again and again to make sure I did not forget what I had learned.

I have tried to pinpoint what made this time with God so much more profound than my other devotional experiences and quiet times. Always before, I had opened God's Word and read it. I had thought about it and even prayed over it, but I had not taken it with me in memory form. Scripture became my vocabulary for prayer as I walked in the morning and even as I moved through the rest of my day.

I had entered a moment-by-moment relationship with God. Dallas Willard believes ordinary believers are designed to live this way.

In his book, *Hearing God,* Willard points to several biblical characters that experienced direct contact with God. Willard says that although we read these exchanges as extraordinary, we should recognize the stories as examples of how any follower of Jesus can and should relate to God.

"God's visits to Adam and Eve in the Garden, Enoch's walks with God and the face-to-face conversation between Moses and Jehovah are all commonly regarded as highly exceptional moments in the history of humankind. Aside from their obviously unique historical role, however, they are not meant to be exceptional at all. Rather, they are examples of the normal human life God intended for us: God's indwelling His people through personal presence and fellowship. Given who we are by basic nature, we live—really live—only through God's regular speaking in our souls and thus, 'by every word that comes from the mouth of God.'"[3]

The Gospel of Luke records a conversation between two ordinary people walking the seven-mile road from Jerusalem to Emmaus. Still reeling from the crucifixion, Cleopas and his friend struggle to make sense of what has happened. The little band of followers experienced enormous pain and loss. Jesus was dead and now something strange had happened. His body was gone. Missing.

Engrossed in discussion and overcome with emotion, they failed to recognize the resurrected Jesus when he matched his steps with theirs and asked them what they were talking about.

" 'About Jesus of Nazareth,' they replied. 'He was a prophet, powerful in word and deed before God and all the people. The chief priests and our rulers handed him over to be sentenced to death, and they crucified him; but we had hoped that he was the one who was going to redeem Israel. And what is more, it is the third day since all this took place. In addition, some of our women amazed us. They went to the tomb early this morning but didn't find his body. They came and told us that they had seen a vision of angels, who said he was alive. Then some of our companions went to the tomb and found it just as the women had said, but they did not see Jesus'" (Luke 24:19b–24).

Do you wonder how two followers of Jesus could miss the truth? They talked and walked with Jesus. Yet, they could not see Him by their side. Perhaps they were so caught up in their own pain and confusion, they missed the fact that He was right there with them and had much to say.

Jesus went right to the point, He said to them, 'How foolish you are, and how slow to believe all that the prophets have spoken! Did not the Messiah have to suffer these things and then enter his glory?' And beginning with Moses and all the Prophets, he explained to them what was said in all the Scriptures concerning himself" (vv.25-27).

When the trio arrived at Emmaus, the friends begged Jesus, whom they still did not recognize, to join them for dinner. Luke describes the moment when it clicked. "When he was at the table with them, he took bread, gave thanks, broke it and began to give it to them. Then their eyes were opened and they recognized him, and he disappeared from their sight. They asked each other, 'Were not our hearts burning within us while he talked with us on the road and opened the Scriptures to us?'" (vv.30-32).

Suddenly everything they had experienced made sense.

I understand what Cleopas and his friend meant by burning hearts. Jesus joined me on the farm trail, and we made the trek together. What I experienced became fire in my bones. A renewed passion overflowed into relationships, work, and ministry. The Holy Spirit took the Word of God and gradually but steadily began changing my life.

Believers are not strangers to trouble. In a close-knit group of Christian friends it is likely someone will be struggling in their marriage. Another family will be in crisis with a child. Someone else will have recently lost his or her job or be forced to deal with a physical problem. Believers have financial difficulties and aging parents. Sometimes we even cause our own suffering.

Perhaps you find yourself in such a place. You may be facing an important decision or reeling from a sudden crisis; or you may be dealing with a difficult issue or a stressful person. As a Christian, you have a vague feeling you should have an answer from God, or at least you should know the next step to take. But you lack direction. You feel stuck and afraid. Your thoughts circle with no relief from the hurt or confusion you suffer. You don't know what to do.

Sometimes a wilderness experience is not dramatic at all. Nothing tragic has occurred; in fact, our life may look the same to friends and family. But we wake up one day and realize we are wandering. Our responsibilities seem routine, even boring. We crave something more. This lack of direction may not look like a crisis, but turmoil still churns our minds and our bodies.

Have you recognized that Jesus walks by your side? He has matched his step with yours. And when you are ready to listen, He will speak the truth that will set you free.

When you consciously move toward God, your experience won't be exactly like that of another person; however, it will be what you need. I have discovered the depth of connection I have with God directly corresponds to the amount of time I spend with Him.

Incorporate Scripture memory into your life. Make it a priority and a pattern of living. Adjust your schedule and do whatever it takes to make it happen. Find the time and establish the place. You will have to make sacrifices to have this kind of relationship with God, and don't be surprised if you feel strange at first. After all, you have entered uncharted territory. Ask God to show you how to begin and then stay with it. God wants to reveal Himself to you. He wants you to know His heart and recognize His ways. Put forth the effort. Whether you are on a trail or in a closet, He will meet you where you are.

If a renewed prayer life and friendship with God were all there was to my story, it would still be worth telling; but there is more—a time when freshly memorized Bible passages became my lifeline in a storm.

3 LEAN FORWARD:
Prepare in Advance

In January 2011, my husband closed his practice and began a new phase of his medical career. This change eventually meant we would relocate to another city. It wasn't an easy decision, and I grieved leaving my job, my friends, and the church that had become family.

I was sad but not afraid. The hours I spent talking to God and memorizing His Word made my relationship with Him as real as my relationship with my husband. I did not wonder if God cared. I did not wonder if He would guide us through this new valley. I knew Him and His ways because we had spent so much time together. I felt His presence, and I could only shout His praises when I realized He had prepared me in advance.

When I think about advance preparation, I go back thirty years to my mother's death. Throughout her two-year illness, my dad taught me a great deal about commitment and sacrificial love.

A few weeks after she died, the church where I had grown up invited Dad to give his testimony. I don't know how he had the strength to stand and share, but he did. Most of what he said that night is a blur, but one comment resonated deeply and influenced my decision making throughout the years. My dad's wisdom: "You don't get ready for illness and death after you receive the diagnosis. All the years you are walking and trusting God, you are really preparing to rely on Him when the dark times come."

God gave me the year on the farm trail to prepare me for the crisis in our lives. I believe if I had not spent the year in Bible verse boot camp, God would have continued to love me and meet my needs; but I would have missed the depth of relationship that developed between us during those holy hours. My relationship with God brought confidence to my soul.

Now my walking and praying took a specific focus. I craved verses reminding me of God's faithfulness and my dependence on Him.

"The Lord is the One Who goes before you. He will be with you. He will be faithful to you and will not leave you alone. Do not be afraid or troubled" (Deut. 31:8, New Life Version).

Lord, You know I don't want to move, but I know wherever we go you will be with us—not just with us, but also ahead of us. I take great comfort in this fact. Help me to be energized, excited, and bold.

Our problem faded into insignificance when compared to what many people endure; however, I have come to this conclusion: whether a circumstance is desperate or merely difficult a believer must make a choice.

In his book *Renovation of the Heart*, Dallas Willard says we focus on the wrong thing. What happens to us is not the issue. "A carefully cultivated heart will, assisted by the grace of God, foresee, forestall, or transform most of the painful situations before which others stand like helpless children, saying, 'Why?'"[1]

We can't always control what happens to us, but we can control how we respond. *What would I do with this unexpected development in my life? How would I behave? Where would I turn for counsel?*

Many times I wanted to complain to anyone who would give me an audience, but I managed to hold my tongue. I had made a commitment. I would focus only on what God led us to do. By God's grace, instead of taking my frustration to other people, I poured out my heart to Him while I walked, prayed, and recited the Scripture I had so recently memorized.

One of the most difficult parts of the experience was the not knowing. Jim and I joked about feeling like Abram and Sarah. We knew we were leaving—we just didn't know where we were headed.

At times, we were tempted to take matters into our own hands. God said to let Him do the leading. We had to learn to wait.

Our waiting wasn't to be passive. In the meantime, we had plenty to do. God revealed a plan for us to follow—neither rigid nor legalistic. The plan would create the opportunity for us to hear from Him and receive what we needed from fellow believers.

We were to begin by changing our perspective.

4 LEAN FORWARD:
Change Your Perspective

I said, *"Your will be done."*
"Do it my way" is what I meant.

Timothy Keller says my problem was not the situation I was in; rather, I struggled because I built my identity on something other than Jesus.[1]

The problem arises when we attach so much significance to something it becomes what we believe we must have to be happy. This something might be a particular relationship, or a career achievement, or some kind of life milestone. In my case it consisted of several good things—solid friendships, connection to church and community, and meaningful work.

Sometimes we think we are seeking God and His plan, but in reality we are attempting to get what we ourselves want. James, the brother of Jesus and the pastor of the Jerusalem church, nailed our problem when he wrote: "You ask and do not receive, because you ask wrongly, to spend it on your passions" (James 4:3, ESV).

To be willing to accept God's plan and not push for our own agenda, we must let go of our perceived right to have something we believe should be ours. To illustrate, I didn't deserve to have friendships that stood the test of time; and I didn't have a "right" to publish a Christian magazine. Those parts of my life, while significant, were gifts given to me by God. I had to let go of these things and my desires concerning them and turn my full attention to Him.

Christians, including me, love to quote Romans 8:28—"And we know that in all things God works for the good of those who love him, who have been called according to his purpose"—as though God is obligated to arrange our lives according to our preferences. We may be willing to compromise on the time frame, but we want a happy ending. We want healing. We want the right job. We want to succeed. We want our kids to stay out of trouble and do well in school. I wanted to stay put.

I thought I had a pretty good grasp of what Romans 8:28 meant. Many pastors and teachers had warned me not to treat God like He was some kind of vending machine in the sky. I knew enough to concentrate on loving Him and His kingdom purposes. I thought God would take my circumstances—the good, the bad, and the ugly—and eventually, if I was patient and tried to live according to His commands, He would save the day. In my situation, that meant Jim would resume his work in some amazing fashion. In the meantime, I needed to pray and watch for the miracle. And I believed I knew what that miracle should be.

Something significant happened in my theology when I went beyond learning individual verses to memorizing longer passages of Scripture. As I walked and prayed through the eighth chapter of Romans, the Holy Spirit showed me how the verses related to one another. To put verse 28 in context, I needed to go backward as well as forward in the passage.

"Now if we are children, then we are heirs—heirs of God and co-heirs with Christ, if indeed we share in his sufferings in order that we may also share in his glory. I consider that our present sufferings are not worth comparing with the glory that will be revealed in us" (vv.17–18).

The apostle Paul offers his readers an eternal perspective on suffering. No matter the difficulty we endure, those problems will be nothing when we compare them to the glory of our future. Right now things feel painful, but one day we will enter the presence of God and what we endured on earth will no longer matter.

Paul moves us to realize that while we wait on perfection—perfect bodies, perfect creation, and perfect relationships—we do not suffer alone. We communicate with God through prayer. Even when we don't know what to ask, the Spirit prays what is in our hearts and somehow, mysteriously, aligns our needs and desires with the will of God.

"In the same way, the Spirit helps us in our weakness. We do not know what we ought to pray for, but the Spirit himself intercedes for us through wordless groans. And he who searches our hearts knows the mind of the Spirit, because the Spirit intercedes for God's people in accordance with the will of God" (vv.26–27).

It was when I pressed forward in the passage, memorizing the verses beyond Romans 8:28, that I had a recognize-truth moment—an epiphany, if you will. "For those God foreknew he also predestined to be conformed to the image of his Son, that he might be the firstborn among many brothers and sisters" (vv.29). I realized I had confused the definition of good with pleasant. To me, good meant happy, productive, safe, and fulfilled. Stated another way, good meant getting what I wanted.

God's purpose has much more to do with the person I was becoming. Working everything for good did not mean He would change the situation; rather, He would use the situation to change me.

Link verses 28 and 29 together, and you will realize God's good work is to shape His children to look like their older brother, the "firstborn among many." God wants me to depend upon Him the way Jesus did. He wants me to treat other people the way Jesus did. He wants me to leave my personal desires behind and allow Him to use me for kingdom purposes—the way Jesus did. God is in the process of transforming each of His children. He will use people, situations, and even the crises of our lives to achieve the results He desires. The best thing I can do is to cooperate with the process.

This principle is easy to understand when you think about your kids. I spent so much time watching my sons play ball I should have a set of bleachers named for me. Being a competitive family, we found it easy to get caught up in the fervor of a particular game or the crescendo of a stellar season. Because I saw so many contests spread out over so many years, I came to realize the outcome of games made little difference in anybody's life. Of course, we all had more fun when our teams won; but the ultimate result of practice and preparation proved far more important than a championship trophy.

Competition taught us all kinds of lessons. For example, an individual is capable of achieving more than he or she thinks possible; positive results require a long-term commitment to hard work and sacrifice; and absolutely, under no circumstances, should a mama yell at an umpire. The possibility of winning kept the boys motivated, but life-changing growth happened during, and because of, the process.

Becoming like Christ is God's expectation of me—His goal for my life. On my own, even with good intentions, the very idea is laughable. But as Andrew Murray points out in his classic book, *Waiting on God*, God knows what He wants from His children, and He has promised to make it happen.[2]

Working on my character didn't seem as if it would be as easy or nearly so satisfying as simply changing the situation. I wanted God to make my life better. I wanted smooth sailing, not a raging sea. But sometimes God sends us into the storm because we need the experience.

The Gospel of Mark records the story. After Jesus fed the 5,000, Scripture says He withdrew to an isolated place to be alone with God. Before He left, He sent the disciples across the lake in a boat, straight into the teeth of a storm. Frantically, the men worked to save themselves. Somewhere between three and six in the morning, Jesus finally showed up, walking across the water. The disciples, exhausted, fearful, and angry, had been rowing against the wind and waves for hours. They had expected Jesus so much earlier.[3]

The answers don't always come when we want them.

Joseph spent more than a decade struggling with the whys of life. Why did his brothers sell him into slavery? Why did his boss's wife falsely accuse him of rape? Why did he end up forgotten, wasting his best years in a dungeon? Imagine his prayer life: "What is the deal, God? I had a dream and I was following you."

We can answer Joseph's questions because we know the end of the story. God had a plan. God worked something good from the events that had seemed so terrible. Eventually, Pharaoh released Joseph from prison and gave him a huge governing assignment. Now second in command, Joseph guided the nation of Egypt through times of prosperity and prepared them for seven years of hardship.

We all know people who achieve fame and fortune rapidly and then quickly self-destruct. Sometimes they take others down with them. Joseph wasn't one of those guys.

From his late teens until the age of thirty, Joseph was deprived of everything a normal person would expect. Now he presided over an entire country. After everything he had suffered, Joseph could have convinced himself he deserved the good life.

Fortunately for the nation of Egypt and Joseph's entire family, he never lost focus. He was prepared for leadership and decision-making because God taught him what he needed to know. While he lived as a slave and a prisoner, God prepared him to govern a kingdom. During those fearful, lonely years, God had refined his character and given him practical experience. Joseph became the man God could use, and then God changed the circumstances and placed him where he needed to be.

Many years later, after his father's death, Joseph reassured his brothers. He would not seek retaliation. Joseph never minimized his suffering, but he pointed to a God who redeemed the situation.

"You intended to harm me, but God intended it for good to accomplish what is now being done, the saving of many lives" (Gen. 50:20).

The shepherd boy, David, also lived some years in the in-between. God chose him to be king of Israel. The prophet Samuel anointed him in an impressive ceremony, but David's family continued to ignore and belittle him. His heroic act—killing the giant Goliath with a sling and a stone—fueled the current king's jealousy. It wasn't long before the young warrior became a hunted man, a fugitive on the run. When things seemed the darkest, David expressed his fears and his faith in beautiful poetry. He poured out his pain and ultimately expressed his confidence in God's goodness and protection. The shepherd boy learned to depend on God. He protected his sheep from wild animals and learned how to fight. For years, he dodged death and became an expert at military strategy. He formed fast friendships and understood the value of loyalty. God taught him courage, perseverance, and obedience. Only then, did David become king.

In the midst of our loss, I asked God to intervene and give me what I wanted. Slowly, Romans 8:28-29 changed my prayers. I could not predict how God would work to bring good out of our situation, but I could already see part of the answer. God intended to develop my character. If I allowed Him to work in the midst of my sadness, I would end up looking more like Jesus. And although it is safe to say I will never rule a kingdom, I have faith to believe God will use my difficult situation to prepare me for future service.

Phillip Yancey, who has written extensively on why Christians suffer, makes this observation. "It should not surprise us that a sovereign God uses bad things as the raw material for fashioning good. The symbol of our faith, after all, which we now stamp in gold and wear around our necks or chisel in stone and place atop our churches, is a replica of a Roman execution device. God did not save Jesus from the cross but 'ironically' saved others through Jesus' death on the cross. In the Incarnation, God's power stream of redeeming good from evil was stealthily underway. God overcomes evil with good, hate with love, and death with resurrection." [4]

Sometimes our painful circumstances become more than a refining fire. While we struggle, God will use our situation to draw other people closer to the kingdom. Paul, the great missionary and apostle, reports what happened while he was stuck in jail.

"I want to report to you, friends, that my imprisonment here has had the opposite of its intended effect. Instead of being squelched, the Message has actually prospered. All the soldiers here, and everyone else, too, found out that I'm in jail because of this Messiah. That piqued their curiosity, and now they've learned all about him. Not only that, but most of the followers of Jesus here have become far more sure of themselves in the faith than ever, speaking out fearlessly about God, about the Messiah" (Phil. 1:12–14, MSG).

Paul's prison sentence gave him a captive audience. Chained between two Roman soldiers, Paul talked about Jesus until the shift changed and then he started over with a fresh audience. Not only did influential palace employees hear about Jesus, but the other believers also watched and drew strength from Paul's behavior. His courage inspired them, and they grew bolder in sharing their faith. Paul recognized the gospel advanced because of his jail time, not in spite of it.

In Acts 16, we see the same pattern in a different story. Paul and Silas had been beaten severely and thrown into the most secure part of the prison—the dungeon. Their feet were shackled, and they were bruised and bleeding. But instead of focusing on the pain, the pair sang hymns of praise and prayed out loud. The Bible says the other prisoners paid attention to their worship, and then God changed the circumstance.

"About midnight Paul and Silas were praying and singing hymns to God, and the prisoners were listening to them, and suddenly there was a great earthquake, so that the foundations of the prison were shaken. And immediately all the doors were opened, and everyone's bonds were unfastened" (Acts 16: 25–26, ESV).

The jailer woke up and made a reasonable assumption: *the prisoners are gone and I am responsible.* He immediately drew his sword to kill himself.

The only thing more surprising than the earthquake was Paul's voice.

"But Paul cried with a loud voice, 'Do not harm yourself, for we are all here.' And the jailer called for lights and rushed in, and trembling with fear he fell down before Paul and Silas. Then he brought them out and said, 'Sirs, what must I do to be saved?'" (vv.28–30).

As a result of all the bad things that happened to Paul and Silas and their willingness to prioritize God's message over their freedom, the jailer and his entire household became followers of Jesus.

Thankfully, these two apostles knew they belonged to Jesus. Their primary desire wasn't to leave a tough place behind, but to use that bad place to share the love of Christ. The events came as no surprise to Paul—he had seen God do the miraculous on many occasions, beginning with his own conversion experience. Paul and Silas didn't have to be comfortable, healthy, or even free to be effective. They were poised to speak and ready to act as soon as they had opportunity.

Like the falsely accused servant, a shepherd on the run, fishermen in a storm, or a missionary locked in a dungeon, the place, person, or situation we beg God to change may be the very experience He will use to make us like Jesus. He uses our pain to prepare us for our future. Our weakness opens doors for other people.

Author and psychologist, Dr. Larry Crabb describes how God shapes our character through difficult situations.

"Desert experiences, those uncontrollable and unpredictable seasons in life when things that used to work just fine no longer work, are good. In the hands of a gracious God, their purpose is to change the questions we ask. Rather than wondering if we're adequate to keep things together and reach our goals, we begin to hear ourselves ask the question our new heart has been whispering all along: 'I love my Lord, what can I give to His purposes?" [5]

Crabb explains this question brings joy to the Spirit and a certain answer to those who are willing to change their focus.

I want God to work in my life, in the hard times and when my way is smooth. I know He is responsible for the outcome—I don't earn my salvation or my growth, but I can cooperate with the Spirit as He refines and shapes, chisels and molds. This cooperation is not a legalistic, rigid set of rules but a way to a deeper relationship. This relationship with God is where every good thing will happen.

5 LEAN FORWARD:
Eliminate Distractions

In 1988, my husband and I had a preschooler who loved music and a *Sesame Street* video filled with great tunes. We played the video so often we memorized it all. Our favorite part was when Ernie and Mr. Hoots, the owl, performed a high-energy rendition of "You Gotta Put Down the Duckie If You Want to Play the Saxophone."[1]

Even our three year old understood the logic behind the song. *Sometimes we have to let go to move ahead.*

If you knew Jesus would visit your town tomorrow, would you cancel your tennis date to see Him? Would you call your boss and ask for the day off, and perhaps invite her to come along, too? Would you change your hair appointment or miss the big game? Exactly what would you put aside to get yourself to the feet of your Savior?

Jesus promised He would never leave us or forsake us. He walks with us down the grocery store aisle and sits with us at our desk at work. Take confidence in His presence, but realize the joy comes when you make the effort to meet Him directly and intentionally.

Before I went to kindergarten, my mother read to me every day after lunch. One of the books we both enjoyed was a sweet story with simple illustrations. *If Jesus Came to My House*, written by Joan Gale Thomas, captured the joy of a child anticipating a visit with his friend.[2] If this wonderful event occurred, the two would play with the child's best toys. If Jesus came to his house, they would share a snack. If Jesus came to his house, they would play in the garden.

The little boy imagines Jesus to be about his age and size and is eager to share all his nicest toys with Him. He wants to make Jesus feel comfortable, and anticipates he will have nothing to fear with Jesus right beside him.

Jesus wants to have that kind of contact with you. In fact, He stands at your front door, attempting to get your attention.

"Here I am! I stand at the door and knock. If you hear my voice and open the door, I will come in and eat with you, and you will eat with me" (Rev.3: 20, New Century Version).

This passage has been used so effectively in evangelistic invitations that many believers don't realize the words are spoken to people who already know Christ. Jesus is telling them they have grown so busy with activity they have lost their passion for Him. He wants to share His wisdom, but He is waiting for an invitation to dinner.

We know the sacrifices we make and the distance we travel when things matter to us. While in college, I camped out overnight to buy tickets to the NCAA National Championship. People wait in line for hours to buy the newest technology or to see the latest movie. To snag a bargain, Black Friday shoppers arrive at stores before daylight. I know some students and a few adults who spent most of a weekend in a Chick- fil-A parking lot to win a year's worth of free chicken sandwiches. We willingly, even eagerly, adjust our lives based on decisions that what we want is worth the investment.

Many believers have been inoculated against "kingdom passion." We have heard just enough about Jesus to know we are supposed to love Him, but we lack the zeal it will take to push past our worries and own agendas to really build our lives around our Savior.

The biblical writers used phrases of intensity to describe a relationship with Christ. Words like "panting" and "desire" speak to our need for Jesus. But rather than race to his arms, we run to other things—work, accomplishments, hobbies, and activities.

Many of us have a strong work ethic, and we're addicted to the sense of accomplishment. We fling around to do lists with pride and make sure other people know how busy we are at work, at our kid's school, or even volunteering at church.

The routine of our ordinary existence can be the very thing that keeps us from life transformation.

We prefer immediate gratification to the on-going effort a relationship of intensity requires. Often we settle for good enough until something painful or difficult grabs our attention.

Perhaps you made a bad decision and must deal with the consequences, or someone harmed you and you now suffer from the emotional or physical injury as a result. You may have lost a person you loved. Satan could be attempting to derail your life at a time when you are about to be used by God for an amazing purpose. God may be preparing you for a greater assignment by testing you.

The "why" doesn't matter as long as the difficulty pushes you to know Jesus. You can speak with the Creator of the universe before you do the laundry or leave for work. You don't have to climb sycamore trees or push through crowds to touch His robe. You don't have to camp out in a parking lot or wait in line, but you do need to answer the door.

God calls to us from the pages of Scripture, inviting us to taste and see that He is good. God spoke to Moses through a burning bush and to Elijah in a still small voice. Dallas Willard says we become so preoccupied we likely would walk right past the fire.[3] I know I have missed the whisper because I've been so busy expressing my own point of view.

In the parable of the four soils Jesus explains the difference between merely hearing and really listening. We can hear God's Word with our ears; but if the truth never penetrates our hearts, nothing about us will be any different.

Jesus said when we fill our time and our thoughts with possessions, career, or even family and friends, we become like the thorny soil. The seed falls into the dirt and begins to grow, but the thorns take over and eventually choke the plant.

"The seed that fell among thorns stands for those who hear, but as they go on their way they are choked by life's worries, riches and pleasures, and they do not mature" (Luke 8:14).

In times of crisis, anxious thoughts may become our new normal. Our minds go from point A to point B and then to point C, which takes us right back to point A. When we wake up in the middle of the night, we realize our subconscious repeats the same loop it made the previous afternoon. Unless it is broken by the grace of God, this thought pattern continues to feed our anger, fears, and hopelessness. *The breakthrough occurs when we spend consistent time with Him.*

For over thirty years, Steve built his career. Finally, he assumed the helm of a successful corporation. An ethical concern came to his attention and he had to make a choice: please a board of directors or follow God's instructions. Steve decided to resign his executive position rather than compromise on the issue. He experienced the predictable emotions—grief over missed opportunity and anger over what had occurred. He struggled to understand why God allowed this to happen, and then he wondered what to do next. Did God have another plan for him so late in his career?

Steve quickly realized he needed to give God time to speak to him. He rearranged his priorities so he could detect the Father's voice.

"These are little things, but they helped me so much. I listened to Christian radio throughout the day. That meant I turned off my sports talk and focused on what God might be telling me through the teaching and the music. I set aside a specific time to pray and read the Bible each day. I used a little devotional book and it seemed every day something from either the radio programs or my devotional reading was sent to me from God."

During this time Steve began to think differently. "I knew my anger could block me from hearing from God, so I began to pray for the people who had harmed me. As I prayed for them, I quit dwelling on their actions and instead asked God to work in their lives, just like I wanted Him to work in mine."

"My prayer life grew deeper as I prayed for God to show me what to do. I realized He was leading me to do a personal inventory. What had I done to contribute to the problem?"

Sometimes we miss God's voice because of what is going on inside of us. We hurt and so we seek to deaden the pain. We fail to go deep to that place of introspection where God can tell us about ourselves, showing us our sins and failures. We fail to understand why we keep making the same mistakes.

God will teach us how to be content in all circumstances. He will meet every need we have, but we have to admit our complete dependence on Him and face the problem. Many times it's easier to eat a doughnut, go shopping, or play another round of golf than it is to stand honestly before God.

Jesus says that our fruitfulness depends upon our listening. We have to be receptive to His teaching and leadership. The only way we will hear is to turn loose of some things that feel comfortable. We must push past the distractions.

In my college communications class I was introduced to diagrams that visually demonstrated what happens when people attempt to communicate with each other. Interruptions in the communication process, known as noise, garble the message.

Noise distracts. Noise interferes. Noise prevents the receiver from understanding what the sender of the message wants to communicate.

The noise could be external: a baby crying when mom and dad are examining bank statements or a teen texting in the backseat of the car while her parents are trying to discuss her falling grades. Noise could be internal such as thinking about a lengthy to-do list that makes it difficult for us to really listen when a lonely neighbor wants to talk.

Noise also prevents us from hearing God. Some noise—like the television in the background—has been with us so long that often we don't recognize it as a problem.

Frequently, noise is enjoyable. God wants us to enjoy good times, but when we fill all our waking hours with media and hobbies, we may miss Jesus knocking at the door.

If you desire to hear from God on a moment-by-moment basis, you must lay the groundwork. This requires regular time alone with God in a quiet place where you can be honest before Him. It also requires a listening heart. You need to know God intimately, so you recognize His voice. God wants to talk to you about your problems, your plans, and your potential, but He probably won't compete with Facebook or your workouts at the gym.

In his letter to the Philippian church, the apostle Paul communicates his one great desire. He says he wanted to know Jesus and to be like Jesus. He let go of everything else in his life to grab hold of his Savior.

"But whatever were gains to me I now consider loss for the sake of Christ. What is more, I consider everything a loss because of the surpassing worth of knowing Christ Jesus my Lord, for whose sake I have lost all things. I consider them garbage, that I may gain Christ and be found in him, not having a righteousness of my own that comes from the law, but that which is through faith in Christ— the righteousness that comes from God on the basis of faith" (Phil.3: 7-9).

A passionate existence isn't without sacrifice; but it is rich and fruitful, filled with purpose and meaning. Knowing Christ is worth any schedule adjustment you have to make. Jesus stands at your front door now. Ask Him inside. Clear the clutter off the couch and invite Him to stay awhile. He will help you with the distractions in the kitchen or the thoughts in your head. Ask Him to prepare the soil of your heart to receive His message. Be still and wait.

You gotta put down the remote control if want to hear a word from God.

6 LEAN FORWARD:
Confess Your Sin

At the age of eight, I engaged in a full-fledged cover-up. Actually, my initial mistake was unintentional, and if I had owned up right away the consequences would have been minimal. But like a Watergate operative, I didn't consider confession. That's when the real trouble began.

About a year earlier, the doctor said I might benefit from reading glasses. So my parents made the financially significant purchase. At first, the pink, cat-eye-design made me feel glamorous. Gradually, however, the eyewear became more of a nuisance than a fashion accessory. I wore them sporadically; but because of my mother's insistence I always had them with me at school—just in case. Monday through Friday, she opened my black patent leather purse to make sure I had everything I needed: a dime for milk, three sharpened pencils, and of course, the glasses.

The day began innocently enough with all the normal checks and balances. Sometime around noon—lunchtime for Miss Dickerson's third-grade class—a strange occurrence set a cycle of events in motion that forever changed my life. I wore my glasses to the cafeteria.

When I sat down at the table with my friends, I unwrapped the usual peanut butter and jelly sandwich and absentmindedly stuffed my glasses into the brown bag. When the bell rang, we filed back to class. On the way out of the cafeteria, I threw away my trash.

It was late afternoon when I sat down at the dining room table to begin my homework. I opened my purse to retrieve a pencil and realized my glasses were not where they were supposed to be. Immediately, I knew what happened. My stomach hurt. I completed my spelling and planned the deceit.

The next morning I pretended to be sick. Since I never stayed home from school, Mama was sympathetic. She let me spend the rest of the day on the family room sofa and even brought me lunch on a tray. I didn't utter a word about the glasses or my deception. I spent that day dreading the next. The ruse would soon end, and I would have no choice but to admit the truth.

Sometimes we end up in difficult places because of our own choices. We blurt out something with an edge and hurt another's feelings. We spend money and hide it from our spouse. We don't want to admit our failure so we attempt a cover-up. We choose. We decide. We hide. We pretend. We are responsible.

As a young child, Michael was sexually abused by a relative and began to act out almost immediately. His mother recognized his unusual behavior, but chose to hide it from his father. Michael says appearance didn't match his experience. "Others believed our family was in great shape. Church was a part of my life, but both religion and family life felt rigid and superficial."

At age eleven, the boy discovered pornography. By the time he was fifteen, he was sexually involved with several girls.

He graduated from high school and just wanted to get away from home. "I enlisted in the Marine Corps. With all my physical needs met, I had plenty of disposable income that I spent on beer and acting out sexually. My idea of Christianity said I was already going to hell—I might as well enjoy the trip."

Eventually Michael became so sick of his lifestyle he realized he had to make a change. "My mom had written to me on several occasions. She knew I was having problems, so she always included the phone number of a Christian ministry designed to help people like me. I didn't know what else to do. I made the contact."

An Army captain called him almost immediately. The officer's willingness to spend time with Michael humbled him. "Here I was — a Lance Corporal — a peon, who bought women and had a drinking problem. This captain was everything I was not. He was successful. He had a healthy marriage. He was a good father."

The captain and his wife brought the young man into their home and included him in their lives. They picked him up for church and even loaned him their car to come back and forth when they were away.

"I wanted to be like him," Michael says. "I wanted what he had. He showed me so much grace that he led me to Christ."

The captain introduced Michael to the chaplain on base who encouraged him to attend AA meetings. Michael says his life began to turn around. "I gave up alcohol. I knew the strip clubs had to go. I began to mature so much spiritually that I left the Marines and entered a Christian college, where I met Laura, the woman who would become my wife."

The Gulf War interrupted college, and since Michael served in the Marine Corps Reserve, he received a call to duty. For a brief time, he saw action. Laura wrote to him every day.

Michael finished his military commitment, returned to school, and asked Laura to marry him. She had already graduated from college and begun the first year of medical school. When she accepted Michael's proposal, she also changed her career plans. He explains her decision. "I was going to be a preacher, and she didn't see how she could make the physician/preacher's wife combination work. Laura entered nursing school, and six months later we were married."

Life should have been rolling along pretty well at this point. The couple loved each other. They were pursuing career goals, building a home together, and serving God. Michael was studying to be a minister and had a part time job at a church. But a significant problem came to light.

The young man had used every ounce of his own willpower to move beyond his addiction, but pornography still had a stronghold on Michael's life.

Laura was devastated when she first discovered the porn. She knew about her husband's past, but Michael admits he had selectively packaged what he told her. Now she felt she had been duped. She began to question her faith and their relationship. Michael explains the pain his wife carried. "She saw my pornography addiction as her failure. She carried such great shame she would never admit it to anyone. She buried it all and just told me to stop."

Michael says they eventually went to a counselor, but neither of them had the courage to admit what was happening, so they left with no insight or help. "I kept getting busted with the porn and just got tired of worrying that the church would discover my problem, so I dropped out of the ministry. I quit my job and decided I would be a counselor."

He says he graduated from school and found a good job. The shadow of porn hung over the marriage, but the couple pretended it didn't exist. "Our solution to my addiction had been to move—to start over somewhere new. With a fresh start, we believed we could leave the past behind. We never dealt with the problem."

He says he frequently prayed prayers like this: *Lord, please help me. I have sinned. I know it looks bad, but I promise if you will get me off the hook this time, I will bear down extra hard and do better. I will read my Bible, pray, and go to church. Really, I don't want to do these bad things, and I don't want anyone to be hurt as a result of my actions. So, please don't let anyone find out about this. Seriously, I'm not trying to avoid anything; I just don't want people to be hurt.*

He prayed with all sincerity. He asked God to remove the desire. He enlisted all his willpower to change, but he did not admit his problem to anyone else.

"My perception of confession was that it was about punishment. I never realized that in God's economy, confession is about intimacy and fellowship. Confession equals freedom."

Although the reason for our shame may be different, most of us can relate to Michael's struggle. Because the process of confession opens the door to restoration and relationship, Satan actively works to prevent confession from taking place. He causes us to believe we would be rejected if anyone ever found out what we had done. He attempts to shame us into isolation.

In a recent message, my pastor, Jason Spears explained the difference between guilt and shame. "Guilt says I made a mistake. Shame says I am the mistake."

When we feel shame, we don't see how God can accept us in spite of Christ's death on the cross. We define ourselves by our failures. Like Adam and Eve after the fall, we attempt to hide from God.

Shame means we live in fear of being discovered. We would never voluntarily admit our failures to other people because we think we are the only one who has ever done something so bad. We believe others don't struggle like we do. We convince ourselves that our friends at church would not associate with us if they knew what we did and how we thought. We define ourselves by what we have done.

If Satan can't derail you with shame, he will use pride to block your relationship with God and other people. Pride murmurs to us about our own goodness. Pride keeps us from ever really seeing our sin.

The Pharisees diminished their own sin and hardened their hearts to the truth of God. Their pride even seeped into their prayers. They would never recognize what God was saying because their ears were filled with their own self-justification. They sang their own praises and failed to recognize their true sinful condition.

"The Pharisee stood by himself and prayed: 'God, I thank you that I am not like other people—robbers, evildoers, adulterers—or even like this tax collector'" (Luke 18:11).

We do the same thing when we dismiss our sin as inconsequential. Intellectually, we know we think wrong things, say wrong things, and do wrong things; however, we don't often take inventory of our own lives. We fail to consider how our sin distances us from God and other people. Jesus called us to examine our hearts.

"And why worry about a speck in your friend's eye when you have a log in your own? How can you think of saying to your friend, 'Let me help you get rid of that speck in your eye,' when you can't see past the log in your own eye? Hypocrite! First get rid of the log in your own eye; then you will see well enough to deal with the speck in your friend's eye" (Matt. 7:3–5, New Living Translation).

When we close our hearts to conviction, we remain removed from the pain we cause. We treat our sin lightly, so we don't feel the need to confess. Satan uses pride to make us like the older brother in the parable of the prodigal son. We live graceless lives in judgment of other people while at the same time we fail to recognize our own lack of love. When we distance ourselves from our sin, we hide behind the walls of pride we constructed to protect our reputation from assault. We define ourselves by what we don't do.

Both shame and pride distort the truth, but God's answer is the same for all of us.

First, we must experience true conviction of our sin. Conviction happens when we invite the Holy Spirit to take God's Word and apply it to our situation.

We must enter the pain of our sin. Like King David, we begin to see our sin as real. We realize we do not deserve mercy, but we can live forgiven and restored lives because of the death of Jesus.

"Have mercy on me, O God, because of your unfailing love. Because of your great compassion, blot out the stain of my sins. Wash me clean from my guilt. Purify me from my sin. For I recognize my rebellion; it haunts me day and night. Against you, and you alone, have I sinned; I have done what is evil in your sight. You will be proved right in what you say, and your judgment against me is just" (Ps. 51:1–4a, NLT).

We find freedom when we make a shift in the way we see ourselves. We are no longer concerned about what others think about us. Instead, we desire to please God with all we say and do. This is the first step to a new way of living. Confession of sin lifts the burden of fear from our shoulders. We don't ever have to worry about God's response.

The teachers of the law and the Pharisees brought a woman caught in adultery to Jesus. They made her stand before the group and then they accused her, not because they were concerned about the law, but because they wanted to trap Jesus.

Our Savior didn't have the reaction they imagined, so the men continued to badger him for some kind of response.

"They were trying to trap him into saying something they could use against him, but Jesus stooped down and wrote in the dust with his finger. They kept demanding an answer, so he stood up again and said, 'All right, but let the one who has never sinned throw the first stone!' Then he stooped down again and wrote in the dust. When the accusers heard this, they slipped away one by one, beginning with the oldest, until only Jesus was left in the middle of the crowd with the woman. Then Jesus stood up again and said to the woman, 'Where are your accusers? Didn't even one of them condemn you?' 'No, Lord,' she said. And Jesus said, 'Neither do I. Go and sin no more'" (John 8:6–11, NLT).

Our Savior's response lifted the woman out of her sinful lifestyle and gave her a new way of thinking about herself. After this encounter with Jesus, the woman caught in adultery knew she had *made* mistakes but she *was not* a mistake. By the grace of God, she could now walk free and sin no more.

Richard Foster says the first step to a different life is an accurate assessment of our current condition. "Honesty leads to confession and confession leads to change."[1] We don't have to wonder or worry if God is willing to forgive us even if we have brought the same thing to Him a thousand times before. When we agree with God about our sin, which is the true definition of confession, He is ready to listen and forgive. The blood of Jesus Christ paid our debt, removing any reason for us to live with the shadow of sin hanging over our lives.

When we confess our sins we must also relinquish our rights. We are no longer determining our steps—God will guide. We are no longer keeping the problem to ourselves, afraid of what other people think. Scripture instructs us to confess our sins to another believer.

"Confess your sins to each other and pray for each other so God can heal you. When a believing person prays, great things happen" (James 5:16, NCV).

Believers need a trusted Christian brother or sister who will consistently speak the truth of God into their lives. If we try to pretend, that person will call our bluff. If we try to hide, that person will shine the light of Christ into our situation. Michael's freedom began when he found a Christian counselor and began to share the truth of his situation. "At the point of my confession, when I finally moved past all the manipulation and lies, I began a journey of accountability and healing. I began to invite people into my life to help me and to hold me

LEAN FORWARD: CONFESS YOUR SIN

accountable. At first Laura didn't believe I was changing. But about 18 months into my recovery she recognized I was a different person. The porn was gone." Today he has structured his life so that men who love him and speak truthfully to him surround him. They hold him responsible for his actions; and because of that accountability, he is able to be the kind of husband and father God him created to be. Michael returned to the ministry, and instead of hiding his past, he shares his story. He tells anyone who will listen that God's grace can free anyone from the clutches of addiction.

Confession removes the barriers Satan works to erect. If we really understood what confession brings to our lives, we would use every ounce of energy to bring our thoughts and actions out of the darkness and into the light. Confession pries open closed hearts and allows us to experience the promises of God. Confession pulls down all pretenses and binds our heart to Christian brothers and sisters in the way God intended us to live. Relationships resume. Broken lives become whole again.

I have taught Bible study groups for many years. My teaching resonated with others, not when I hid my faults, but when I spoke honestly about my own sin and struggles. God has designed us to learn from each other, but we will never have the opportunity if we live behind walls of pride or shame.

There were many times in my childhood when I made bad decisions, disobeyed, and did things my own way. Some of them I remember, many I have forgotten. But the great glasses cover-up stands sharp and clear because of how I felt before I confessed, and what occurred when I finally came clean.

I had been miserable for a full day. As an eight-year-old girl, I didn't know what made me devise such a complicated lie. Today I understand my motivation. I was not afraid of discipline because I lost the glasses; rather, I did not want to admit I was capable of being so irresponsible. In my effort to protect my reputation, I lied. I believed losing my glasses would change my parents' perception of me.

When Mama opened my purse that morning, I cried tears of regret. My explanation of my deceit tumbled out, and I experienced her grace. She loved me anyway. Regret turned to relief, and then relief became joy.

I don't remember the consequences I suffered for my behavior. I am sure they were appropriate because we didn't get away with much at our house. I do remember what it felt like to be forgiven and restored. In that forgiveness I found a new kind of freedom. I didn't always have to be right. I was a kid, and kids lose things. When I messed up, I needed to admit the mistake, sooner rather than later. Sometimes something could be done to correct the problem, but whether or not the situation could be remedied, I always knew my parents loved me. Their love flowed from our relationship, not from my behavior.

Jesus told the story to His followers. The wayward son left home and squandered his inheritance. Finally, because he was destitute and had no other choice, he headed home. He intended to confess and ask to be a servant in his father's household. The scene Jesus paints is one of the most memorable in Scripture because we understand exactly what is taking place. The son's confession opens the door to complete forgiveness and restoration. The father doesn't hold a grudge, lecture, or demand some kind of restitution. He opens his heart and throws a party.

"The son said to him, 'Father, I have sinned against heaven and against you. I am no longer worthy to be called your son.' But the father said to his servants, 'Quick! Bring the best robe and put it on him. Put a ring on his finger and sandals on his feet. Bring the fattened calf and kill it. Let's have a feast and celebrate. For this son of mine was dead and is alive again; he was lost and is found.' So they began to celebrate"(Luke 15:21–24).

When you don't know what to do, look into God's Word and ask Him to bring you to your senses. Admit your failure, your part in the problem, and the pain it caused. Don't hesitate, deny responsibility, or try to clean yourself up before you come to God. *Confess your sin. Get the party started.*

7 LEAN FORWARD: *Forgive*

You have an enemy. It's not your boss, the IRS, or the guy who sold you that lemon of a car. Satan wants to undermine your relationship with Jesus, and he will launch his attack when you are the weakest and most vulnerable.

The Deceiver has twisted truth since the Garden. He began by creating doubt: "Did God really say, 'You must not eat from any tree in the garden?'" [1]

He continued by whispering lies: "You will not certainly die," the serpent said to the woman. "For God knows that when you eat from it your eyes will be opened, and you will be like God, knowing good and evil." [2]

He sneers, "They took advantage of you."

He strokes, "You didn't do anything wrong."

He sighs, "You will never forget."

Satan's goal is to steal your joy and prevent you from fulfilling God's purpose.

When you refuse to forgive another, you put out the welcome mat and invite the Devil in for tea.

Paul reminded the believers in Ephesus to patch up disagreements as quickly as possible.

"When you are angry, do not sin, and be sure to stop being angry before the end of the day. Do not give the devil a way to defeat you" (Eph. 4:26–27, NCV).

Getting Rid of the Gorilla details Brian Jones' personal journey from anger to forgiveness. He describes a terrible event that occurred in his early adolescence. Beaten by a gang of older teens and betrayed by the criminal justice system, Jones' deep emotional pain continued to haunt his relationships and thinking for many years.

Jones believes when someone harms us, it is natural and rational for us to feel anger. Our challenge is to push past the initial response.

He says it this way: "We couldn't help getting angry when we were hurt; we had no choice in the matter. We can, however, make a decision about whether we'll allow that anger to turn into rage. That is a decision we do have control over. Anger is something that happens naturally; rage is something that we help manufacture."[3]

Rage makes us vulnerable. It feels good to soak in our misery, so we hit the replay button and go back over the details in our mind.

Trey and his wife had been married for 15 years when he discovered his wife was having an affair. He confronted her with the evidence. She admitted her guilt, promising to break the relationship off immediately. She said she would be a different person.

Trey says Christian counselors taught him that getting angry over the sin was a good thing. Jesus became angry when He saw the temple moneychangers making God's house a circus. Righteous anger should occur when a person injures someone else. From Jesus' example, we see that righteous anger prompts action.

"I learned it was okay to experience anger and to express those feelings, but I could not sin in the process. I could not hold this against her."

Trey determined he would forgive, and the forgiveness would be independent of his wife's decisions and future actions.

He explains, "I did not want this terrible thing to define my life. It was also a question of my obedience. There is no doubt we are commanded to forgive in Scripture. I knew I had to let my anger go."

In the biblical context, forgiveness includes the idea of a debt being eliminated as if it had never existed, or someone being released from an obligation. When a person forgives, he or she says good-bye to any right for retribution or payment of any kind.

The act of forgiving does not necessarily put the relationship back together again. One person cannot achieve reconciliation; however, one person can forgive and thereby open the door to reconciliation.

When you forgive another person, you say the individual owes you nothing—no money, no contrite explanations, no apology—not one thing. You set them free from the need to make you happy or satisfied.

The process of forgiving enables you to receive the direction you need from God. You are open and ready. Bitterness will not block the road to joy.

Forgiving isn't easy. In fact, many would agree forgiveness is impossible without the supernatural work of the Holy Spirit.

Trey believes his ability to forgive came from his dependence on God.

"At one time I was sure I would never trust my wife again, but trusting her was not the issue. I had to choose, with God's help, to live in freedom. Every day, sometimes multiple times a day, I would pray and release my right to be angry."

He says that private, personal worship made forgiveness possible. "I replaced painful thoughts with a focus on God's promises and what He had done for me."

If someone has harmed you, you will not feel like forgiving the person; but in submission, aware of how much God has forgiven you, you begin the journey. When you feel the anger rising, you deliberately turn your attention to God.

Trey says he prayed God would bring about the highest good from the rubble of his marriage.

"I didn't want to waste all this pain. The best thing that could happen wasn't that everyone would know I was wronged. The best thing wasn't for me to extract revenge. The highest good would be if my girls had a front row seat to see a life changed by God. For that to occur, I knew I had to forgive."

No one expected Stephen to forgive his murderers in such dramatic fashion. The New Testament book of Acts records Stephen's amazing story. He had shared his faith with passion and eloquence, outraging his audience of religious leaders. "When the members of the Sanhedrin heard this, they were furious and gnashed their teeth at him. But Stephen, full of the Holy Spirit, looked up to heaven and saw the glory of God, and Jesus standing at the right hand of God. 'Look,' he said, 'I see heaven open and the Son of Man standing at the right hand of God.' At this they covered their ears and, yelling at the top of their voices, they all rushed at him, dragged him out of the city and began to stone him. Meanwhile, the witnesses laid their coats at the feet of a young man named Saul" (Acts 7:54–8).

Stephen didn't retreat from his testimony or beg for mercy. In the midst of the horrific crisis, he turned his attention to the Savior he had defended. Jesus stood to welcome him into the eternal presence of God.

Even as they took his life, Stephen prayed for his attackers, "'Lord Jesus, receive my spirit.' Then he fell on his knees and cried out, 'Lord, do not hold this sin against them.' When he had said this, he fell asleep" (Acts 7:59b–60).

Stephen echoed what Jesus cried from the cross. "Jesus said, 'Father, forgive them, for they do not know what they are doing'" (Luke 23:34a).

Gordon McDonald believes Jesus forgave from the cross because He needed to keep His own spirit free from bitterness.

In his book, *A Resilient Life*, McDonald says, "Perhaps it sounds offensive to say, 'If I could get into the head of Jesus . . .' but I'll take the risk. If I could get into the head of Jesus I'll bet I'd find that He was aware that forgiving his enemies was a proactive defense against any temptation to become embittered toward them. If we embrace the truth that Jesus was fully God and fully man and thus capable of facing all temptations (as is said in the book of Hebrews), then I think we're watching a Savior who is protecting Himself against the temptation of hatred and resentment."

McDonald continues, "Jesus did not wait until angry feelings began to cripple His soul; He chose to proactively forgive (or pray for their forgiveness) so that He could remain the sinless Christ who could die for the sins of the world."[4]

When we feel we have been taken advantage of or wronged in some way, one of the most significant things we can do is to ask God to show us our own hearts. He will reveal our pride, our self-righteousness, and any other sin we may be harboring. When we see our own failure, we are more likely to approach forgiveness as Christ commanded.

Believers attract attention when they suffer and yet choose to focus on God. People expect us to lash out, sink in despair, or just give up. They don't expect peace and confidence. We look most like Jesus when we choose to forgive.

Make the decision to release anyone who has harmed you from the need to say they are sorry. When you free them, you free yourself. God receives the glory, and others want to know more about the source of your strength.

No matter how someone has sinned against you, with God's help, you can forgive. Forgiveness begins with a decision to follow God and not your feelings. Forgiveness continues with great intention, on a moment-by-moment basis, as you take each negative, critical thought to God in prayer.

Use the book of Psalms to give voice to your feelings. David and the other writers certainly didn't package their words into socially acceptable requests. They poured out their hearts. They trusted God to handle the situation.

When we cry out to God, He hears us and gradually leads us out of our turmoil. If someone has sinned against you, put the consequences in the hands of God. He sets you free to love and forgive.

As you release the person from what he or she owes you, you will find yourself in a supernatural place—living right in the middle of a miracle. Satan wanted to use another's actions to destroy you, but by God's grace, you practiced what Jesus lived and taught and what the apostle Paul said to do.

"Do not be overcome by evil, but overcome evil with good" (Rom. 12:21).

There is a condition of the heart that makes forgiveness possible. No matter your situation, you are able to move forward with confidence because you have taken the time to remember where you have been.

8 LEAN FORWARD:
Practice Gratitude

I met Doug Kidd in the summer of 2010. He and his pretty wife, Kodi, believed sharing their testimony was part of God's plan for their pain. So, they agreed to an interview with *Wiregrass Christian Magazine,* a publication I edited and published at the time. When we spoke, the forty-four year old husband and father of two had been living with ALS for ten years. ALS (Amyotrophic lateral sclerosis), commonly known as Lou Gehrig's disease, affects all the voluntary muscle groups. It is always fatal.

At this point in his illness, Doug lay confined to bed and could not move or even speak without the aid of a computer, which he operated with the pupils of his eyes. Breathing and feeding tubes kept him alive. Kodi juggled caring for Doug, parenting two teenagers, and her full-time job.

Anticipating a somber atmosphere, I braced myself for the meeting. The moment I entered Doug's bedroom, I knew I stood on holy ground. The man radiated joy and energy.

Slowly Doug typed his story. "In ten years I have gone from a physically strong man—healthy in every way—to someone totally paralyzed, bedridden, and dependent on others for my care." He ticked off the facts of his disease, not because he wanted pity, but because this was the truth of his situation. But in spite of all the losses he suffered, Doug believed God was moving in his life.

"I had to lose control, so God could take control. I rededicated my life to Christ on December 24, 2003. It was a very intense experience. I was shown the kingdom in a special and personal way. I am a new and saved man today, by God's grace. ALS was the way God reached my heart."

Even with so many limitations, Doug viewed each day of life as a gift from God.

"I was supposed to be dead five to seven years ago. Praise the Lord! He has given me five more years to celebrate my children's birthdays, five more anniversaries with Kodi, five more years to celebrate our Lord and Savior's birth and resurrection. He gave me a chance to be saved and be an inspiration to others. I don't think ALS has crippled me. It has given me a chance to be a stronger, better, and more complete man. God strengthens and fortifies me daily through prayer and His Word. My favorite verse now is one my daughter gave me. '*Be joyful in hope, patient in affliction, faithful in prayer.*'[1] That will definitely get you through a rough spot! I love and live that verse every day."

Since that conversation with Doug, I have spent time reflecting on the significance of gratitude in a believer's life. Doug had no control over anything that happened to him. Yet with the only movement he had at his disposal, he praised God. He was grateful for the good gifts he had—a wife and children who loved him, kind caretakers who attended him after Kodi went to work, and most of all, a relationship with God that gave him confidence in his future and purpose for each day. Doug's faith grew even as his physical health declined. He believed more strongly in the God who loved Him, the Savior who gave His life for him, and his eternal home in heaven.

Faith flourishes in the rich soil of gratitude. The Gospel of Luke [2] tells the story of the ten lepers who came to Jesus for healing. The group of outcasts stood far away and cried for help. Jesus instructed them to go and show themselves to the priest. As the group obeyed they found themselves healed—all ten of them. The disease that had controlled their lives and isolated them from other people had disappeared.

Luke records what happens next.

"One came back, praising God in a loud voice. He threw himself at Jesus' feet and thanked him — and he was a Samaritan. Jesus asked, 'Were not all ten cleansed? Where are the other nine? Has no one returned to give praise to God except this foreigner?'"

Jesus wonders aloud at the lack of gratitude the other nine exhibited. Where were they now? When Jesus addresses the grateful man, he says something interesting. "Rise and go; your faith has made you well."

The man's faith, expressed through his gratitude, was the conduit for the miracle. Since Jesus has already brought physical healing at this point, He must have been speaking about something in addition to what had already occurred. In some manner, the Samaritan's healing was greater than the healing of the other nine lepers. The Samaritan's gratitude gave Jesus the opportunity to do a more complete work in his life.

Living with gratitude requires specificity of thought and conversation. Jesus hears our vague pleas, but loves it when we think carefully enough about our petitions to be specific.

When blind Bartimaeus[3] heard Jesus was close by, he called to him and asked for mercy. The plea was passionate but vague and Jesus asked for more information. "What do you want me to do for you?"

It was only when Bartimaeus replied, "Rabbi, I want to see" that Jesus gave him sight.

When we bring unambiguous requests to God, we are more likely to recognize His work on our behalf. The recognition that our prayers have been answered fuels our praise.

One tearful morning I undertook a search for some specific direction from God. Of all places, I found the word I needed in 2 Chronicles, chapter 20.

Jehoshaphat, King of Judah, was having a terrible day. Three enemy armies led by powerful kings made plans to wage war against the nation. God's people found themselves surrounded, out-numbered and out-gunned, so to speak.

Jehoshaphat didn't roll over and play dead. Nor did he run ahead and try to fix this problem on his own. He brought the people together and led them as together they all cried out to God:

"We don't know what to do; we're looking to you" (2 Chron. 20:12b, MSG).

Jehoshaphat reminded the people that God could be trusted. He prayed out loud, naming the attributes of God: holiness, sovereignty, and power. God knew all those things about Himself. God didn't need a recitation of His character, but Jehoshaphat must have realized he and the people needed to remember who God is and what He can do.

The Bible calls this rehearsing. I like the image of the word—saying something again and again until the words are fixed in your memory.

The king led the people to rehearse how God had cared for them throughout their history. The people trusted God for their future because they recognized His protection and provision in their past.

Jim and I walked through our time of transition with confidence in God, not because we liked what was happening, but because we had seen His faithfulness in so many ways. Our young adult children thrived. God gave them summer jobs and wonderful professional and personal opportunities. We looked back in our own lives and recognized God provided for us even before we knew what was ahead.

One year earlier, our house wasn't even on the market when a real estate agent contacted us and asked if we would consider selling. Although the offer caught us by surprise, we decided to take advantage of the opportunity.

We didn't have a place to live, but God provided more than an ordinary home. He gave us a wonderful year on the farm where we grew closer to each other and to Him.

Any time either of us found ourselves drifting into doubt, we would rewind our thoughts and conversation. We rehearsed what God had done.

In the midst of the fear, Jehoshaphat and the people fell on the ground and worshipped God. Scripture says the musicians in the crowd stood and sang praises with all their might.

"With all their might . . ."

What a sight that must have been—the people stretched out before God, begging for His help. Others moved about, singing and playing instruments as if their lives depended on Him.

Don't miss the passion. These folks were focused and called out to God with great intensity. Nothing was half-hearted or casual. What God said and did mattered more than anything around them. I suspect their desperation heightened their awareness of God's presence as well as their absolute willingness to obey.

God desires the same precise kind of thought when we voice our gratitude. If we fail to be specific, not only do we rob God of the praise He deserves and desires, we also lose the opportunity to change the way we think.

The apostle Paul says a lack of gratitude leads to idolatry and causes unproductive thought.

"People knew God perfectly well, but when they didn't treat him like God, refusing to worship him, they trivialized themselves into silliness and confusion so that there was neither sense nor direction left in their lives. They pretended to know it all, but were illiterate regarding life. They traded the glory of God who holds the whole world in his hands for cheap figurines you can buy at any roadside stand" (Rom.1: 21-23, MSG).

Time and again the children of Israel turned their attention away from God, only to be caught up in the world around them. They quit saying thank you to God and no longer recognized God as Giver of everything good. As they shifted their focus to themselves and the world they lived in, their thinking grew warped and unproductive.

I don't relate to idols made of wood or stone, but I do identify with chaotic thinking patterns. When I enter a difficult time, my thoughts bounce from one thing to another. Phrases like "my mind is running in circles" or "I have lost my focus" show up in my thoughts and conversation. My thinking grows cloudy, and I vacillate when making decisions.

This kind of unproductive thinking is a symptom of my personal modern day idolatry. When I prioritize anything else—accomplishment or career, recreational activities or my family or even the idea that I could control my own life—I fail to focus my attention on God. I think about acquiring or achieving or maintaining this other thing more than I think about Him. I no longer view my very physical existence or the circumstances that surround me as a gift from God.

When I recognize my sin, I have a choice to make. I can continue to drift away, locked in the faulty thought processes, or I can return my focus to my Creator, my Redeemer, and the Giver of every good and perfect gift.

When life progresses according to our plan, expressing gratitude feels natural. When darkness comes—and at some point it will come to all of us—giving thanks to God is not so intuitive. When we struggle, God doesn't give us a pass on gratitude. In fact, it seems that at such times Scripture becomes more emphatic.

"Be cheerful no matter what; pray all the time; thank God no matter what happens. This is the way God wants you who belong to Christ Jesus to live" (1 Thess. 5:16–18, MSG).

God doesn't need our expressions of thanks, and we know all His commands are always for our good and His glory. He does, however, want us to give thanks in every situation.

My recent personal experience is teaching me more about God's design for praise. God wants me to name my specific blessings. I praise Him for my salvation, a husband who loves me, Christian parents who took me to church and taught me about God, healthy children, and a comfortable place to live. My list is lengthy. Even the act of naming the blessings causes me to change the way I think. But I have discovered something deeper. As I thank God for the gifts He has given me, I become more aware of the character of the Giver. I know Him better because I recognize His work in my life. When I pause to name specific blessings, I am really pausing to worship; that worship nourishes the relationship I have with Him.

Sometimes however, our present reality overshadows our thoughts of gratitude. When things are so bad we don't want to give thanks, it is good to remember we aren't the first ones to feel this way. In the Old Testament God told His people to go backward in time and think about His provision and His leadership, His power and His love.

When you are struggling today, God wants you to look back at yesterday. When you remember what He did for you in the past, your faith for the present will grow stronger. You will rehearse—revisiting His care for you, His faithfulness, and His grace in your life until your outlook changes. You replace despair with joy when you dwell on what God has already done.

When King David brought the ark to Jerusalem, he gathered the people of Israel together for worship. David instructed the worship leaders to recount God's faithfulness throughout history.

"He remembers his covenant forever, the promise he made, for a thousand generations, the covenant he made with Abraham, the oath he swore to Isaac. He confirmed it to Jacob as a decree, to Israel as an everlasting covenant: 'To you I will give the land of Canaan as the portion you will inherit.' When they were but few in number, few indeed, and strangers in it, they wandered from nation to nation, from one kingdom to another. He allowed no one to oppress them; for their sake he rebuked kings: 'Do not touch my anointed ones; do my prophets no harm'" (1 Chron.16: 15–22).

The book of Psalms is also rich with examples of remembrance. Many times the writer begins with a list of all the terrible things that are happening. They don't minimize the deep feelings of darkness and the questions they have about their situation.

"I cried out to God for help; I cried out to God to hear me. When I was in distress, I sought the Lord; at night I stretched out untiring hands, and I would not be comforted. I remembered you, God, and I groaned; I meditated, and my spirit grew faint. You kept my eyes from closing; I was too troubled to speak. I thought about the former days, the years of long ago; I remembered my songs in the night. My heart meditated and my spirit asked: "Will the Lord reject forever? Will he never show his favor again? Has his unfailing love vanished forever? Has his promise failed for all time? Has God forgotten to be merciful? Has he in anger withheld his compassion?" (Ps.77: 1–9).

The psalmist is in the darkest of times, feeling so far away from God that he had no comfort. He was trying to reach God but the despair he felt only increased.

He wondered what he had done to make God angry. Then he reaches back into history and remembered what God did to bring His people out of slavery.

"Then I thought, 'To this I will appeal: the years when the Most High stretched out his right hand. I will remember the deeds of the Lord; yes, I will remember your miracles of long ago. I will consider all your works and meditate on all your mighty deeds.' Your ways, God, are holy. What god is as great as our God? You are the God who performs miracles; you display your power among the peoples. With your mighty arm you redeemed your people, the descendants of Jacob and Joseph" (Ps.77: 10–15).

In this particular psalm, as well as many others, there is a progression from despair to praise. The psalmist experienced on a personal level what the Israelites felt as a nation. It is the movement all believers share—the journey from the slavery of sin to the freedom found in Christ. This journey and the way God has protected, guided, and provided along the way is what we should remember. Then, we too will raise our voices in gratitude.

It is what Jesus told us to do. "The Lord Jesus, on the night he was betrayed, took bread, and when he had given thanks, he broke it and said, 'This is my body, which is for you; do this in remembrance of me.' In the same way, after supper he took the cup, saying, 'This cup is the new covenant in my blood; do this, whenever you drink it, in remembrance of me'" (1 Cor. 11:23b-25).

Rehearse and remember. I thank Jesus for taking my punishment on the cross and for bringing me into right relationship with God. My gratitude also extends to the life He gives—eternal and abundant. Heaven is my ultimate destination, but Jesus promised He will never leave or forsake me as I travel through this difficult place. Every good thing I experience, every person I love, and every person who loves me is a gift from God.

God meets us in our suffering and gives us what we need. Something powerful occurs as we express gratitude for His faithfulness and His good gifts to us.

When we praise God in our darkness, we join Doug Kidd and others like him—ordinary men and women who found joy in this world and healing in heaven. When we live in gratitude, we live in triumph. We are not perfect people, but our lives are focused on God and His glory. We don't have to do more, try harder, or be better. We just have to come to the feet of Jesus and say thank you.

Now the transformation will begin.

9 | LEAN FORWARD:
Do the Next Thing

If we want to know God's will for tomorrow, we must follow His plan for today. Dallas Willard has said the person who intends to will what God wills begins with what God has made clear.[1]

Obedience doesn't mean we have to be perfect, but it does mean we make a conscious decision to examine our behavior, words, and attitudes to determine if they line up with what God tells us in His Word. It means we respond to the Spirit's promptings on a moment-by-moment basis.

In times of indecision, we fear the worst. Paralyzed by uncertainty, we don't know how things will turn out. We don't have answers to overwhelming problems. It's tempting to quit—to give up doing anything at all.

Francis Chan says believers find it expedient to use not knowing as an excuse for not doing. He writes in his book *Forgotten God*, "It is easy to use the phrase 'God's will' for my life as an excuse for inaction or even disobedience. It's much less demanding to think about God's will for your future than it is to ask Him what He wants you to do in the next ten minutes. It's safer to commit to following Him someday instead of this day." [2]

We dread what obedience might bring to our lives; so instead of doing what we know God desires, we distance ourselves from the source of all wisdom and guidance.

Pharaoh, the Egyptian king, agreed to free the Hebrew slaves and then changed his mind. He refused to do what God commanded, and the Bible says God hardened his heart. When we walk with God, our hearts are tender and open to the things He wants us to know. When we refuse to do what we know is right, our hearts grow colder and less receptive to God's direction.

God emphasized the connection between love and obedience when He prepared the Israelites to enter the Promised Land.

"Listen, O Israel! The Lord is our God, the Lord alone. And you must love the Lord your God with all your heart, all your soul, and all your strength. And you must commit yourselves wholeheartedly to these commands that I am giving you today. Repeat them again and again to your children. Talk about them when you are at home and when you are on the road, when you are going to bed and when you are getting up. Tie them to your hands and wear them on your forehead as reminders. Write them on the doorposts of your house and on your gates" (Deut. 6:4–9, NLT).

Not too long ago I heard a young pastor preach a sermon on obedience. Jonathan Gulley said God wants us to follow His commands just like parents want their children to follow the rules. Wise moms and dads won't let their kids get away with sporadic, half-hearted, whining obedience. They want their kids to do what they ask and do it "quickly, completely, and cheerfully."

When a parent asks a teenager to do something, the kid will frequently go into stall-as-long-as-I-can-and-maybe-they-will-forget-about-it mode. The teen may believe he will actually follow-through at a later time, but mom and dad know otherwise. Stalling is a default position, and tomorrow never arrives.

Or a teen might agree to the parent's direction and mow the grass in the front yard; when dad leaves to run errands, the kid disappears as well. Perhaps a friend called with a too-tempting invitation, or perhaps he simply decided to just get by—do the minimum it would take to satisfy mom and dad.

This kind of limited obedience can be more frustrating for a parent and more difficult to correct than when a child totally refuses to follow instructions. Sometimes children do just enough to convince themselves they have obeyed.

And then sometimes the child performs the assignment but whines and complains so much you wish you had never asked him to help.

I believe one reason God placed us in families is so we can internalize truth about our relationship with Him. The primary reason I wanted my children to obey was not because I wanted the work completed. In most instances it would have been easier to do the task myself. I wanted them to obey because I knew the lessons they learned would be important in their adult lives. What they did today determined what they would do tomorrow.

When a preschooler disobeys, the parent worries about the child's physical well-being and rushes to correct the behavior. When a two-year-old throws a tantrum in the store, the wise mom might get tired of the kicking and screaming, but she doesn't take the lack of self-control personally. The parent expects impulsive behavior because the child is so young. In the teen years, disobedience is more painful. It is more than broken curfew or an ignored request. Disobedience indicates a lack of respect for the parent and a disregard for the relationship. Jesus said our obedience reveals our love for Him. The ones who love Him will also be the ones who know Him.

"Whoever has my commands and keeps them is the one who loves me. The one who loves me will be loved by my Father, and I too will love him and show myself to him" (John 14:21).

When we hit an impasse—a place where we need God's direction, it makes sense to do a self-inventory. Am I following what I know to be truth? Am I doing the last thing God told me to do? Am I doing it quickly, completely, and cheerfully? Have I delayed my response to God? Have I done just enough to get by, to assuage my feelings of guilt? Have I done what was necessary but complained and whined about it the entire time? Or have I given God the kind of obedience He desires?

God doesn't withhold information from me that I need. He longs to have the kind of relationship with me that allows me to understand His ways and to recognize His voice.

We have to be careful when we reflect on the topic of obedience. The Pharisees stressed obeying the law and ended up pushing people away from God. Obedience is not an *I do this for God and He does that for me* way of living. Rather, a lifestyle of obedience reveals the condition of my heart. Jesus said obedience to the law could be summed up with the two greatest commandments. Love God with everything you are and all that you have. Love your neighbor as you love yourself.

Obeying God puts us in the place where we can hear what He is saying. We recognize His voice in a difficult circumstance because His is the voice we have been following all along.

God has handed down some pretty specific instructions. Feed the poor. Give thanks in everything. Show mercy. Use spiritual gifts to build the church. Share our faith. Take care of widows and orphans. Don't gossip. Don't lie. Practice humility.

Sometimes we already know what God wants us to do, and we just don't want to do it. So we run from the truth and keep asking Him for more direction. God called us to work with children on Sunday morning, but we prefer to hang with adults, so we keep looking for a different way to serve. We pray diligently for a new job while we perform poorly at the one God has already provided. The Holy Spirit prods us to call and apologize, but we decide to wait, rationalizing, things will surely smooth over soon.

When we continue to ask God for guidance and we already know what He has commanded, we put distance in the relationship. We move away from God's truth, slinking toward sin and failure. Refusing to act on what we already know to do opens our mind to the possibility of sin. When we hesitate, pushing God's command aside for a later time, we move away from God and the guidance He has to give. It becomes easier and easier for Satan to derail us. Sin is crouching at the door.

"Do the next thing." Elisabeth Elliot, well-known Christian teacher and writer, made this expression famous when she spoke about her decision to remain in the jungles of Ecuador.[3] It was 1956 and she and her husband, Jim Elliot, were serving as missionaries in this hostile place. When Auca Indians murdered Jim and four other missionaries, Elisabeth chose to remain in the jungle and continue the work. Later Elliot lived and worked among the very people who had killed her husband.

She said she often felt overwhelmed with grief and responsibility. She knew she could not do everything she needed to do and the temptation was to panic, collapse, and do nothing. She explains how she was able to function in the difficult circumstances. "I had a good many new roles, besides that of being a single parent and a widow. I was alone on a jungle station that Jim and I had manned together. I had to learn to do all kinds of things, which I was not trained or prepared in any way to do. It was a great help to me simply to do the next thing."

When the "next thing" appears insignificant we may be tempted to ignore God's prompting. God's call could be as simple as sitting with a friend who has lost a child, or taking a casserole to a coworker who just had surgery. When my mother was diagnosed with a brain tumor, one of her friends came to our house and did laundry and mopped floors while we were at the hospital. A clean house didn't cure mother's illness, but it made our family feel loved. My mother's friend did what she could. It was her next thing to do.

At times, doing the next thing means performing a simple task that just needs to be done. We can pray while we wash dishes, change a diaper, or cut the grass. We slip into routine and our thoughts aren't so muddled. On the other hand, the next thing might be to seek God's wisdom in some quiet place completely away from work or friends and family.

Sometimes the next thing is to tell someone you are sorry for what you said. You can't fix the problem, but you can express your regret and as it happens, your words ease the tension and the healing begins.

The next thing might be to make a call and set an appointment to see your pastor or a counselor. God will use the insight you receive to bring you new direction.

And sometimes going to a party is the next thing to do.

For several years we had been taking two young friends to church. Brenda and her younger sister Bianka were faithful attenders. The girls' father had abandoned the family and their mom worked seven days a week to provide for the family, so church gave them a needed outlet for friends and spiritual growth.

In January 2011, Brenda startled me with a question. She was turning fifteen and planning a quinceañera to celebrate her birthday. (Quinceañeras are important occasions in the Hispanic culture. The event begins in church and is followed by a huge party with plenty of food, dancing, and symbolism.) Brenda wanted to know if we would be a part of the celebration, especially Dr. Jim. She wanted him to assume the role of her father.

Humbled by the request, we circled July 2nd on our calendar.

The month of May was hopeful. We knew Jim's initial contract would end on June 30th, but since we anticipated renewal we were optimistic. In the middle of June, we realized Thursday, the 30th, would be Jim's final day at work. By the time it arrived, we were tired and sad. But we couldn't sit and worry—we had a birthday to celebrate.

The preparations were in full swing—fancy food for two hundred people, a perfect dress for Brenda, and now the rehearsals for the father-daughter dance. God used Brenda's big event to bring joy to our lives when we needed it the most.

Consider the biblical account of Ruth. The penniless young widow left her home and accompanied Naomi, her despondent mother-in-law, to Bethlehem. They caused a stir in town, giving local gossips plenty of ammunition. Without male protection or provision, the women were desperate and dependent on God. They needed a miracle.

Ruth didn't have much experience following God. She had zero career options and she certainly could not see the big picture, but she got busy and did what she could. After getting Naomi settled, the young woman cheerfully went to the fields to glean. This was hard and humble work, only made possible by the kindness of the landowner. Thankful for the opportunity, Ruth followed behind the harvesters and collected the grain that remained on the ground.

"So Ruth went out to gather grain behind the harvesters. And as it happened, she found herself working in a field that belonged to Boaz, the relative of her father-in-law, Elimelech" (Ruth 2:3, NLT).

As it happened . . .
These are beautiful words that express the way God often works in our lives. We come to a tough place where losses pile so high we can't see over them. Problems

are too complex. Our past is too troubled. The grief is too profound. We won't recover without the grace of God. We know we need Him, but until the miracle occurs we wonder what we should do.

Ruth moved past loss and fear, and while she waited on God to complete the big picture, she followed the part of the design she could see. She did the next thing.

Ruth went to glean and ended up working in the field of her kinsman. Ruth and Boaz fell in love and married. Ruth gave birth to Obed, the child who filled Naomi's heart with love and graced her arms with responsibility. As it happened meant God planned it all along, for from the marriage of the wealthy Jew and the beautiful immigrant comes the greatest king who sat on Israel's throne. And from the line of David, came Jesus—King Eternal, Messiah and Savior who fulfills the plan God had from before the beginning of the world.

Sometimes we are so far from God we can't imagine ever hearing from Him again. We made the bad decisions that put us in the darkness. The effect of our sin spilled over into the lives of people we love, leaving a trail of broken relationships and shattered dreams.

If you have given Satan control, he won't easily release the hold he has on you. The Enemy wants you to live in fear and confusion. He wants you to feel guilt and shame every day of your life.

There is no time to waste. Run to Jesus. Don't drag your feet or try to figure things out before you go. The One who loved you enough to die for you, has forgiven you and will give you another opportunity to obey God's call.

You will be in good company. Abraham, Moses, Peter, and the apostle Paul all struggled at some point in their lives. Even when they sinned in dramatic fashion, God didn't give up on them. God brought each back to a place where they could obey His call and bring Him glory.

Jesus stands ready to guide you out of the pit of despair. You won't be perfect, but as you follow the Spirit's promptings, you will find peace, joy, and the strength you need to do your next thing.

10 LEAN FORWARD:
Connect with Believers

Go to Church or the Devil Will Get You! The vividly illustrated sign sits in plain view of Interstate 65, somewhere between Montgomery and Birmingham, Alabama. I'm not sure the message has ever reached the lost or inspired the faithful, but it has been good for a few laughs. Last year we stopped and took a photo that our college-age son promptly posted on Facebook.

Growing up, I didn't need a billboard to remind me about church. Sunday morning, Sunday evening, Wednesday night—our attendance was as natural as breathing. I watched my parents share meals, teach classes, make time for ministry, pray for other people, and give their financial support. The commitment was authentic; but since involvement was a way of living, sometimes going to church felt more like family culture than a shared, passionate walk of faith.

Then Mama got sick, and I realized agape love was more than a word from a Sunday sermon.

People came to pray over her and sit with us at the hospital. They brought chicken casseroles and angel flake biscuits and anything else they could think of to show their concern.

With our wedding date approaching, Jim and I considered postponement or scaling back the celebration; but Daddy insisted we keep everything as we had planned. Our large church wedding would give Mama something good to anticipate. I was twenty-three years old, working a new job, and getting married in six weeks. My mother was recovering from brain surgery and I didn't have the slightest idea of what to do next.

The church ladies came to the rescue. Not only did these dear people host beautiful parties and bridal teas, they picked up the scattered pieces of the wedding puzzle and filled in all the gaps. Although they didn't turn water into wine (not allowed at a 1980's Baptist reception), God used them to bless us with a wedding miracle. They told me not to worry about a thing and proceeded to change our dreary church fellowship hall into a beautiful garden, perfect for photographs. They prepared trays of delicacies. They looked for every opportunity to make our wedding a special event, and they did it all with love and grace.

A few months later, another group of church friends organized a transportation schedule so Daddy didn't have to leave work to get Mama back and forth to undergo her daily radiation treatments. For four weeks, these friends took her to every appointment and waited with her at the hospital. If she felt like it, they took her to lunch or on a picnic at the park. Their love was deep and true, cultivated through the years of serving and sharing life like family.

When Dad's job took my parents to a new city in another state, I wondered what would happen to their support system. Although my parents could not attend regularly, their new church immediately became involved in their lives. People visited. They sent cards and notes of encouragement. They showed up with meals and other practical kinds of assistance.

On one occasion, Daddy took a business trip that coincided with one of Mama's many hospitalizations. I traveled to stay with her while he was away. The hospital discharged her after a few days. Even though we celebrated going home, I faced a dilemma. I knew no one in Louisville and needed assistance to get her into the house. Daddy called the church office, and one of the ministers came to help. Together, we were able to carry my mother inside the house and make her comfortable. These church people barely knew us, but they loved God. He had given them tender hearts.

When I was growing up, Mama used to say she had no idea how people traveled through loss without a church family. What I experienced in those days of personal grief confirmed two things I had been taught. Jesus is sufficient for my needs and will be there to walk with me through suffering, and God uses His people to bring His healing into the lives of hurting people.

It was that way from the beginning. The first believers naturally gravitated toward each other. What they had just experienced was so remarkable and exciting it would have made no sense to live this new kind of life in isolation. Jesus changed everything. Now they had a relationship with God, not a religion with a list of dos and don'ts. No longer did they grasp at being good enough to reach God. Jesus, who had been crucified for their sins, was alive. The Holy Spirit resided inside their hearts and brought them a new kind of passionate, purposeful life— an eternal, abundant life to be lived in community with others who were also redeemed by Christ's blood and guided by the voice of God.

These people weren't perfect. They had prejudices and worried about getting their fair share of the resources and attention. They squabbled, and doctrinal problems would require the leaders' attention from time to time. For example, James, the half-brother of Jesus, the pastor of the Jerusalem church, and the Spirit inspired writer of the New Testament epistle that bears his name, said the believers needed to put feet to their faith, stop favoring the wealthy and influential, and keep their mouths shut—or at least place their tongues under God's control.[1]

But in spite of their problems, their focus on the resurrection of Jesus Christ and the way they cared for each other distinguished them from others. The love they showed constituted a strong magnet that attracted all kinds of people to this new, radical faith.

In his book, *Life Together*, Dietrich Bonhoeffer says this kind of meaningful fellowship is not something we orchestrate. He says, "Christian brotherhood is not an ideal which we must realize, rather it is a reality created by God in Christ in which we may participate."[2] We enter into this life when we make the decision to love sacrificially, to minister alongside another, and to walk with our Christian brother through times of need and pain. He points out that this kind of fellowship is truly a gift from God. Not all believers have the opportunity to meet together—they are held apart because of political persecution and imprisonment. When we realize what we have been given, living in community seems more precious, a gift we should not take for granted.

Unfortunately we don't always give others access to our lives. Many of us who attend church hold people at an emotional and sometimes physical distance. Perhaps we fear ridicule or rejection, or maybe it hurts our pride to be honest about our needs and failures. Perhaps we don't want to enter the messy business of caring for another person.

Jesus ministered to huge crowds but cultivated close relationships with a few chosen men. For three years, the friends traveled together and spent hours in conversation. They shared meals and laughter. They wrestled with profound questions. Even though Jesus was fully God, He was also fully man and needed His friends, particularly when He faced the cross.

When they gathered in the upper room to share the Passover, Jesus craved the love and support of His friends. "And he said to them, 'I have eagerly desired to eat this Passover with you before I suffer'" (Luke 22:15).

Later that night the eleven remaining disciples accompanied Jesus to Gethsemane. Jesus went to prepare Himself for the suffering soon to follow and took his closest friends—Peter, James and John—with him farther into the garden. Although the trio fell asleep at this occasion of great emotional pain and spiritual significance, Jesus seemed to need their physical presence. He wanted them close by while He struggled and prayed, aligning His will with God's.

Mary Beth Davis longed for close community. Already an active member of a church, she felt the need to forge a deeper relationship with a few people who could walk with her through a difficult time. She called three Christian women and invited them to join her for lunch. Although each knew the other, at this point they weren't close friends. Two had only recently moved to town.

Lunch began with casual conversation. After a while, Mary Beth explained the purpose of her invitation. "I am going through a divorce and I have just lost my job. I need a support system of women who will pray for me and invest in my life. I want to do the same for you and wonder if you would be that kind of friend for me."

Mary Beth took a risk. Her vulnerability gave others the rare opportunity to begin a purposeful friendship. It doesn't matter what people have or don't have in common. If they share in Christ, He gives meaning to their relationship.

The apostle Paul asked his friends for help. Sometimes he needed practical things—his coat and his papers. Sometimes he asked for specific prayer. During a time of significant depression, God sent someone to encourage him:

"When we arrived in the country of Macedonia, we had no rest. We had all kinds of trouble. There was fighting all around us. Our hearts were afraid. But God gives comfort to those whose hearts are heavy. He gave us comfort when Titus came" (2 Cor. 7:5–6, NLV).

I remember the day I returned to work after Mama passed away. I had been coping pretty well, keeping my emotions under control for the sake of my grandparents. It seemed strange to leave a world filled with pain and grief and walk right back into an office environment and pretend nothing had happened.

That's the way I wanted to act that day—as though nothing had happened. I feared losing control if anyone said anything about my loss, so I remained businesslike and aloof. One person penetrated my loneliness with her love.

Peggy, a colleague and Christian friend, insisted on taking me to lunch. She asked a couple of questions and then sat and listened to me talk. I don't remember what I said at all, but I remember the empathy she extended. Peggy provided a safe harbor for my feelings. Her kindness lifted me out of the deep darkness and reminded me of God's limitless love. I don't think I would have ever reached out to anyone at all had she not been there to initiate the healing conversation. She served me by listening.

Now and then we need a brother or sister in Christ to speak God's Word to us. We read the Bible and believe what it says; but when we enter a season of doubt and difficulty, we need to hear someone else speak truth into our lives. I may need reassurance about heaven or God's love for me. I may need someone to remind me that God is my Strong Tower, my Redeemer, and my Friend. I may need someone to tell me again that Jesus sits at the right hand of the Father and intercedes for me right now. When I can only muster a tiny bit of faith, I need another to bolster my confidence by speaking of his or her convictions.

At those times, when we don't know what to do, we find it easy to focus on ourselves. We quit thinking about what other people are going through. Yet, the best thing for us to do would be to forget about our own problems and get busy ourselves serving alongside another believer.

Jesus said it this way: "If anyone wants to keep his life safe, he will lose it. If anyone gives up his life because of Me, he will save it" (Matt. 16:25, NLV).

Just a few years ago, Renee made a difficult decision. She left a successful career in the corporate world to move back home. Her parents, now much older, needed help with their small business. They also required assistance with doctor visits and everyday life. The emotional abuse she had suffered as a child in their home made Renee's decision more difficult. When she left after high school graduation she had promised herself she would never come back; but thirty years later she found herself returning home to care for the parents who mistreated her as a child.

She says it took a great deal of prayer to be willing to do this thing God called her to do. She believes the reason she went back is because her parents exhibited a new receptivity to the gospel. As they grew older, they seem to be searching for spiritual answers. She believes God called her to be with her parents in their final years in order to lead them to Christ.

After Renee returned home, she became involved with a local church. She attended Bible studies and corporate worship on a weekly basis. In addition, she participated in a variety of ministry projects. She made hospital visits. She paid special attention to elderly people shut in at home or residing in a nursing facility. She served as a kind of ministry connector for people in her church and the community at large. Renee says she found strength and purpose in her relationships with other believers. She built community with others as they served together. These relationships fortified her to continue her ministry to her parents, who remained distant and critical.

Years ago Jim and I lived in Decatur, Alabama. I participated with a group of women who gathered weekly for Bible study and prayer. The Spirit knit our lives together as we prayed for each other and ministered together.

Recalling how we served together, one particular experience comes to mind. A couple that attended our church adopted six little girls, ages two to six. At the time, their older brother was only seventeen. The mother unexpectedly came down with a serious illness. The timing could not have been more difficult, since the father had recently taken a new job in another state. The mother was hospitalized immediately, leaving the teenage boy at home to care for his six little sisters.

Our group of ladies found out about the situation and went to work. We created a schedule and arranged for the girls to be with one or two of us every day as long as the mom remained in the hospital. We planned tea parties and roller-skating. We brought the girls to church with us and they made our carpool runs with us in the afternoon. We often played tag team and handed them off to a friend in the middle of the day. We made sure the children got their meals, their naps, and their baths, and enjoyed a good time in the process. We wanted the girls to feel secure and loved, as though they were attending summer camp with good friends, instead of worrying about their mom in the hospital. Eventually, their mom recovered and family life returned to normal. The girls' dad came to collect them all and move them to their new home.

Several years passed. Then unexpectedly, one day the family returned to our church. Three of the children had made decisions to follow Christ. They wanted to be baptized and share this special occasion with the church family who cared for them all those years ago.

When you don't know what to do, go to church. Go frequently to the prayer meetings, the ministry events, and the picnics. Go to the children's programs, even if your own kids left home long ago. You worship, pray, fellowship, and serve with other believers because being together makes a family work. Church should feel like family, but to get to that deepest point of connection takes commitment to one another and an investment of time.

Since we married thirty-two years ago, Jim and I have belonged to four different congregations. Each time we have relocated to another town we always grieved leaving our church family. Seven years ago, when we relocated from Decatur, Alabama, to Dothan, Alabama, I felt certain I would not be able to find a church that I could love as much as I loved those wonderful people in Decatur. Even though I was confident God had a place for us to serve in our new community, I doubted if I would ever again feel as connected to another group of believers.

We set up the beds and unpacked a few pots and pans. Then we began to visit churches.

We asked God to guide us. He led our family to First Baptist, Dothan, a downtown church with a faithful, loving pastor, a strong emphasis on foreign missions, and a commitment to local ministry.

It took some time, but gradually Jim and I found our place. It happened as we prayed and taught Vacation Bible School and drove church vans. It happened in Sunday School classes, on mission trips, and over coffee with our new friends.

Once again, church became family.

When we made the move to Albany, Georgia, we were empty nesters. Without children to encourage connection, the process of getting to know people seemed more difficult. Based on my previous experience, I knew adjusting to a new community would take time and some work. It would be relatively easy to unpack boxes and find the grocery store—the difficult part would be making friends. No matter how busy I find myself, I live with a restless feeling until those relationships develop.

First and foremost, Jim and I knew we had to find our church home. We prayed and asked God for His guidance. This time He led us to Providence Church. We describe ourselves as contemporary, casual, and focused on relationships. Our church bears many similarities to the ones to which we belonged in the past. Our pastor is loving and passionate about proclaiming the Word of God. The church has a strong commitment to ministry.

It isn't easy to begin again, but most growth experiences prove challenging. Throughout the stages of my life, God set me in new places with new people to stretch me, to make me depend upon Him instead of on myself, and to teach me that His Word is true in every situation and every location.

My understanding of church has deepened. Whether I am in Decatur, Dothan, or Albany, I am part of the body of Christ. Because I belong to Jesus, I am also a part of every other person who follows Him. The Holy Spirit binds hearts in a miraculous way, making it possible to put aside personal desires and opinions. All types of believers—people who have little else in common—can come together to live and share like family.

This faith family crosses denominational lines, geographic locations, and racial boundaries. The relationships formed in the name of Jesus resemble no other. In His name, we love, give, and sacrifice. In His name, we struggle together toward a common goal. Because of the way we love, the world will draw closer to God.

I am eager to feel connected again; but in truth, I already belong. The past relationships, the ones I formed with my brothers and sisters in Christ through the years, are a part of who I am today. The ones I will form wherever I am will contribute to the person I am becoming.

So I will smile, walk across a room, and introduce myself. I will ask a question and listen carefully. I will remember names. I will jump in and participate even when I feel like I don't belong. It will take a little work and a little time for us to get to know each other, but because of God's grace, it will happen. I am almost home.

When you look for a church family, you don't look for perfection. You search for people who love and follow Jesus and who are committed to caring for each other. We are, after all, sinners saved by grace. We hurt each other's feelings and miss opportunities to demonstrate love. We will fail and falter and seem far away from what God means for His people to become. But grace offers us all another chance, a fourth chance, a fiftieth chance. Those who recognize how much grace they have received recognize how much grace they need to offer.

Worship, serve, love, and give—be the conduit for God's grace to other people. And when you don't know what to do, tell your pastor or your Sunday School class or one fellow believer. They will listen. They will speak God's truth. They will pray over you. They will help with weddings and new babies and financial difficulties. They will suffer with you, and they will share your celebrations. They will bring you dinner, not because you need to eat, but because they find joy when they show their love.

11 LEAN FORWARD:
Pray with the Kingdom in Mind

Writing about prayer makes me nervous. There are others more qualified to speak on this subject. Those men and women pray more than they talk about prayer. They exhibit peace in stressful times and joy in sorrow. They love when others would retaliate. We call on them to intercede for us because we see the results of their connection with God.

I own dozens of books written by scholars and saints who have taught me about communicating with God. I go back and reread them because I need the inspiration and the teaching.

But in spite of a truckload of disclaimers, I feel compelled to share. In my weakness, God has shown Himself strong. He has accepted my little faith, my distracted focus, my small offerings, and He has blessed and multiplied and poured out His grace in abundance. He has made much from little. I feel like the boy with the loaves and fishes, jumping with pleasure while pointing at Jesus. "All I had was this little lunch, but see what the Master did!"

I saw something funny and couldn't wait to tell Jim. I quickly sent him a text message—laughing out loud as I thought about his reaction. That kind of thing happens when people have a close relationship. Often, when you learn something new, you will want the other person to know about it right then. You will make a phone call, not because you need to communicate information but because simply hearing the person's voice makes you smile.

The Bible says God communicates with His people all the time. He longs for us to know Him. When we catch a glimpse of His heart, we begin to understand just how much He loves us. We bring Him pleasure. We make Him smile.

When our three boys were young, we attempted a family devotional each evening before we put them to bed. It could be a sweet time of sharing. More often there was this strange juxtaposition, a free-for-all punch and tussle backdrop to Bible stories and prayer. Every evening each of us said a sentence or two, thanking God for His gifts or asking for His protection and guidance. I will always remember when our youngest son, the life-full-throttle two-year old, jumped to his feet and shouted out this prayer: "Dear Lord Jesus, the more fun we can have!"

We could debate my son's syntax and theology, but I've had eighteen years to think about it, and it seems to me the little fellow hit on something pretty profound. God wants us to be filled with joy when we think about Him. He delights over us, and He wants us to delight in Him as well. What a grand idea: have more fun—enjoy God more.

"Take delight in the Lord, and he will give you the desires of your heart" (Ps 37:4).

Delight means we long to spend time with Him. We listen and pray and look expectantly for Him at every turn and juncture of our lives, just like we wait on our best friend or our children returning from college. Delighting in God changes the way we live. In the process of loving and enjoying Him, what we want in life, both generally and specifically, aligns with His will for us.

We celebrate His work in and around us. God calls us and changes the way we think. We look forward to spending time with other believers, so we can delight in God together. We find our meaning and our purpose in our relationship with Him, and as that relationship develops, we realize He gives us more than we could ever ask for or imagine. He pours out Himself and His good gifts to fulfill the desires of our heart.

God revealed His glory in creation and His holiness in the Old Testament law. He demonstrated His faithfulness as He provided manna each morning to the Israelites. He gives glimpses of His creative power every time a baby, unique from all others, enters the world. The ultimate demonstration of God's character came in the form of Jesus who lived and died for us, revealing once and forever the extent of the Father's love.

Through our own experiences, God wants us, as His people, to relate to Him collectively and to know Him individually. Jesus describes what happens when we make knowing God our priority.

"If you abide in me, and my words abide in you, ask whatever you wish, and it will be done for you. By this my Father is glorified, that you bear much fruit and so prove to be my disciples. As the Father has loved me, so have I loved you" (John 15:7–9, ESV).

Living with Jesus means your prayers will be answered. You will be able to say, "Look what has happened to me! See what God has done!" People will better understand God's heart because they see the love He has lavished on you. Prayer is the vital link in this kind of expectant living. Without frequent, intimate times with God, we will find ourselves disillusioned—trifling with what is sacred and true.

Jesus went to lonely places to pray. He met God early in the morning, before anyone else made demands on his time. He prayed late in the evening when He felt exhausted from a day of ministry. The Bible tells us He withdrew when He learned that His cousin John had been murdered. He entered into intensive, lengthy times with God before He made big decisions—beginning His ministry, choosing disciples, and facing the cross. Jesus needed to communicate with God. He did not fit God into His life; rather, our Savior built His life around what it took to nourish the relationship with His Father.

He instructed the disciples in prayer. He told them to ask and seek and knock. He said they should be specific with requests and believe God would supply their needs. Jesus taught the disciples to pray for daily provision, forgiveness of sin, and protection from Satan. He taught them to ask God to bring His rule and reign in their lives and world—to ask God to use them to bring heaven to earth.

We know the content of Jesus' prayer for all believers.[1] He prayed for our protection, courage, and strength. He asked God to make us effective and powerful witnesses in the world. Jesus prayed that believers would experience unity with God and with each other in order that the world could see and understand God's love for them.

We also know our Savior struggled in Gethsemane[2] in anticipation of what awaited Him: the horror of the crucifixion and the separation from His Father. Only after agonizing prayer did He come to the point where He strengthened Himself to do the Father's will.

We know God spoke out loud at Jesus' baptism: "And a voice from heaven said, 'This is my Son, whom I love; with him I am well pleased'" (Matt. 3:17).
And at the transfiguration: "A voice came from the cloud, saying, 'This is my Son, whom I have chosen; listen to him'" (Luke 9:35).

In their times together, I believe God must have expressed His love to Jesus. I believe Jesus asked for wisdom to discern God's will and for the strength to do the right thing on a moment-by-moment basis. Perhaps He asked for the patience to deal with dense disciples and know-it-all Pharisees. The time He spent with His Father in the morning equipped Him to fulfill His mission the rest of the day. But Jesus' communication with the Father didn't end when He left the intimacy of the quiet place and moved into the world. What took place in those conversations overflowed in Him and through Him as He ministered, taught, and proclaimed the arrival of the kingdom of God.

When Jesus looked at people, He saw straight into their hearts. At times, He showed outrage at evil. He felt the pain of those who had no direction. He loved the unlovely and brought hope to anyone with the heart to receive Him. He welcomed lonely people and sinful people with open arms. He hugged little children and answered questions with wisdom beyond anything anyone had ever known.

He was God, but He was also man. He limited Himself when He came to earth and was subject to every temptation and trial we have ever experienced. He didn't snap His fingers to deal with the difficulty of life. He lived perfectly because He lived in relationship with God. Through the connection of prayer, the Father's love and guidance flowed to the Son and love and worship streamed from Son to Father.

Jesus tells us we can experience this same kind of life with God. We ask God to help us see things the way He sees them. Suddenly our prayers aren't so neat and tidy. We grieve for a hurting world. We cry tears with Him. We feel joy with Him.

God intends for us to enter the kind of life where we hear Him speak and we speak to Him. This new relationship feels real and passionate, not distant or stuffy. When we make time and space like Jesus did, we will experience the same kind of amazing love that Jesus shared with His Father. Our private communication with God will give us strength and wisdom. And we will find there is really no beginning nor end to prayer. Communication with God will follow us to the grocery store, to work, and to the tennis court. Other people will notice.

Jesus is complex, beautiful, and holy. We can only imagine what it will be like to be with Him forever; however, as we pray, we experience a taste of the relationship that is to come. Communication with God becomes more like breathing and the relationship anything but mundane.

This prayer life is a process and it begins right where you are. How do you begin to delight in Him? Tell God what you love. After all, every good thing that happens to you comes directly from His hands. Then ask Him this question. What does He love? Ask Him to help you learn to love those very same things.

Tell God what you fear or what you need to decide or where you struggle. Ask Him to take care of you, and then thank Him that He will. Ask Him to give you wisdom to make good decisions and then thank Him that He will. Ask Him to show you your heart and your motives. Thank Him for His forgiveness and pray that today, nothing in your life will prevent you from hearing Him. Tell Him how much you love Him, and then ask Him to help you learn to love Him more.

Spend more time listening than talking. Live with the expectancy that God will show up in your life at any moment.

Dallas Willard says believers must learn to live as though God is about to speak. "The reality of God's voice does not make seeking for it unnecessary. When I seek for something, I look for it everywhere. It is when we seek God earnestly, prepared to go out of our way to examine anything that might be his overture toward us—including the most obvious things like Bible verses or our own thoughts—that he promises to be found (Jeremiah 29:13). But we will be able to seek him only if we honestly believe that he might explicitly address us in ways suitable to his purposes in our lives."[3]

In the everyday sameness of my life, I can miss opportunities to see God work. Recently, I was thinking about my day ahead. I had nothing on my to-do list that made my heart beat faster. In fact, I had nothing on the agenda I wanted to do at all. I found myself wondering what it would take to turn the routine into something memorable. I needed a divine appointment—a God-directed encounter with another person. I asked Him to give me that very thing. Standing in line with my grocery cart, I met a young woman who needed encouragement. I would not have recognized the opportunity if I had not already asked God to open my eyes.

Seek God's perspective when you read the newspaper or a co-worker complains about her kids. Perhaps today your prayer will be righteous indignation and outrage at evil. It might sound like this:

You: That is wrong. Somebody should do something.
God: *Good! We're on the same page. I will tell you what to say.*
You: I meant somebody else. Somebody smarter, braver, or more connected. How about Lisa? You know she's always ready for a challenge.
God: *I'm talking to you this time. Are you listening?*

My relationship with my own children taught me more about prayer than I learned from any book or sermon. When they were preschoolers, the kids asked for things all the time—juice, a friend to play with, a new toy. They asked me to do things for them they couldn't do alone. "Pick me up, Mommy," or "I climbed too high. Mommy, get me down."

When they requested and I delivered, I garnered smiles, giggles, and hugs, but when they asked and I said no, I got pouts, complaints, and the occasional tantrum.

Years passed. Now my sons would ask my opinion or request help with a problem. The relationship progressed from "give me" to "teach me." As our three boys became older teens, something even more dramatic happened. They already knew what Jim and I believed. Most of the time, their lives reflected what we expected without the discussion those same kinds of decisions once required.

Now we could experience communication on a new level.

We dreamed together. We asked them questions and shared our insights as they made decisions out of the character that had been formed in them during the first eighteen years of their lives. They still needed our physical resources and an occasional discussion of basic principles. But now the relationship went deeper and became defined more by what we shared—experiences, ideas, and love—than by the tangible things Jim and I provided.

Something similar occurs as we grow in our relationship with God. We begin simply by requesting specific things from the Father who loves us perfectly and has promised to supply our needs. As we spend time together, we find our prayers begin to change. The change reflects the difference in our thinking. Through this process called abiding, as we listen and wait, we discover knowing God has become more important to us than anything else. We pray now with confidence because we know we are praying according to the will of the Father. We pray now with excitement because we anticipate the answer to our prayer. And sometimes, like Jesus, we pray with the kingdom in mind.

12 LEAN FORWARD:
Replace Lies with Truth

I've heard the voice. Perhaps you have too.

"You blew it. You'll never have another chance."
"If you mattered, God would not have let this happen."
"This relationship is hopeless—there is nothing you can do. Get out now."

Sometimes, it's a whisper at the point of temptation. "Go ahead. No one will ever know."

The voice calls from magazine covers and television screens, planting seeds of insecurity and dissatisfaction.

"You're not pretty enough, and neither is your kitchen."
"You'll never be successful, might as well quit trying."
"You are way too old to start anything new."

This voice isn't new. Satan has been speaking lies and discouragement since the beginning of time. He plants seeds of doubt with his taunting.

It is the way the Deceiver works; He wants us to doubt the truth. Satan wants us to question what God has said about us and deny what God has told us to do.

Scripture says John baptized Jesus and then the Spirit led Him into the wilderness. During the next forty days, Jesus immersed Himself in deep communion with God, as He prepared to launch His public ministry and set in motion God's plan to redeem the world. It's no surprise that at the point of such great significance Satan wanted Jesus to question His identity and His mission.[1]

"*If* you are the Son of God, tell these stones to become bread."

"I will give you all their authority and splendor; it has been given to me, and I can give it to anyone I want to. *If* you worship me, it will all be yours."

"*If* you are the Son of God," he said, "throw yourself down." (emphasis mine)

In dramatic fashion, Satan presented the Savior with a way out—easy and spectacular. Jesus recognized Satan's lies because He understood God's plan and purpose. He knew Scripture, and He used the Word of God to counter the Enemy's voice.

"Jesus answered, '*It is written*: Man shall not live on bread alone, but on every word that comes from the mouth of God.'"

"Jesus answered him, '*It is also written*: Do not put the Lord your God to the test.'"

"Jesus said to him, 'Away from me, Satan! *For it is written*: Worship the Lord your God, and serve him only.'" (emphasis mine)

Satan's lies lost their power and attraction in the bright light of truth.

If Satan can appear enticing in the Garden and persuasive in the wilderness, we should expect him to show up in our lives on a regular basis. Frequently, he comes when we are about to make a choice to obey God. We should expect to hear from Satan when we are poised to make a right decision, to follow Christ in service, to sacrifice our own desires, and to advance the kingdom of God.

Throughout Scripture, God tells us who He is. He longs for us to know His heart. He wants us to see how much He loves us. He wants us to obey in faith even when we don't understand. He wants us to follow Him even if we don't know where we are going. He wants us to seek Him out, not to get something we want, but to get something that we need, that is, more of Him.

"To the Jews who had believed him, Jesus said, 'If you hold to my teaching, you are really my disciples. Then you will know the truth, and the truth will set you free'"(John 8:31–32).

We can be free from the chains of repetitive sin and the lies this world tells us. When we hear the voice that calls us to doubt our salvation or our value to God, when we hear the whisper that tells us to give up on relationships, when we grow discouraged and we wonder if we matter at all, we can do exactly what Jesus did. We can use the Word of God to send Satan packing. We can refuse to give the Deceiver access to our minds and our decisions.

The Enemy wants to catch us in a web of fear and anger. He wants us to doubt our decisions and to doubt God's plan. He wants us to give up, shut down, and stay miserable. He wants us to change our focus from God's direction to our own desires.

It's easy to justify almost any feeling we have or action we want to take. We can talk ourselves out of doing the right and good things just as quickly as we convince ourselves it's okay to do the wrong ones. We color the truth with our own preferences. Often, it's a subtle slide. We make several gradual decisions that eventually take us far away from the plan of God.

If left to our own devices we will deceive ourselves. Eventually, we won't recognize our true condition because we've lived with Satan's lies for so long. We believe what he tells us and begin to rationalize our own behavior.

But when believers spend time on a regular basis in the Word of God, we recognize how God works. We can identify His call.

"My sheep listen to my voice; I know them, and they follow me" (John 10:27).

We hear the words of Jesus by opening our Bibles and reading them for ourselves. When we spend more and more time understanding how Jesus lived, taught, and thought, we will recognize His voice in the routine of our lives. We will see the relationship between our situation and what the Bible teaches.

"Grace and peace be yours in abundance through the knowledge of God and of Jesus our Lord" (2 Peter 1:2).

In Peter's second letter, which he likely wrote near the end of his life, he gives the traditional greeting. But these words in verse two are more than just a connection from authorship to content. If more grace and more peace is what we want, Peter tells us the knowledge of God is the route we must take to reach our destination.

The believer does not strive to attain grace and peace; rather, our lives become characterized by growth in these traits when we commit ourselves to knowing God.

"His divine power has given us everything we need for a godly life through our knowledge of him who called us by his own glory and goodness" (2 Peter 1:3).

Verse three explains that we don't achieve this grace-filled, peaceful state by our own efforts. We enjoy the grace and peace of God in the midst of difficult circumstances because the Spirit of God uses the Word of God to transform our thinking. The Spirit of God moves our attention off ourselves and focuses it on what God says.

"Through these he has given us his very great and precious promises, so that through them you may participate in the divine nature, having escaped the corruption in the world caused by evil desires" (2 Peter 1:4).

God wants His children to know Him, but not because He needs our approval. As we better understand His character, we will find the grace and the peace we desire. We will recognize the promises of God and have confidence that those promises are true and for our benefit.

When we begin to know Him, we can identify His plans and purposes, and the way He works in this world. He wants us to recognize what He is doing in our lives now and what He wants to do in the future as we yield to Him. He wants us to recognize the kingdom of God advancing around us, so we can be a part of what He is doing.

When we begin to approach our study of Scripture with a hunger to know God's character, we are beginning a journey into the depths of relationship. The Holy Spirit will use the Word of God to take our relationship with God to a deeper, more satisfying place.

"But when he, the Spirit of truth, comes, he will guide you into all the truth. He will not speak on his own; he will speak only what he hears, and he will tell you what is yet to come" (John 16:13).

Our need pushes us to Scripture. As we read, we open our hearts and minds to see more and more of God's character. We will be encouraged because we know the One who holds our future is trustworthy. We will be able to wait on Him and His timing with confidence. God will teach us a new way to think. We will be transformed by the "renewing of our minds," and in that process of transformation we will discover how to live.

It's what Vicki Martin discovered when her husband of 28 years moved out. She knew Tony had a drinking problem. They had separated several times. The crisis came in May 2006. Tony left for work one day and didn't come home for over a year.

She explains, "Tony said he didn't want to be the person he had become, and he had prayed many times and asked God to change him; but he was still the same. He had come to the point where he believed God existed, but he didn't believe God cared about him, and so he decided he didn't care either."

It would have been easier to give Tony the divorce he said he wanted, but Vicki didn't yield to her own desires or to the advice of well-meaning friends. Instead, she turned to her Bible, searching for answers.

For many years, Vicki had been a serious student of the Word of God. She attended Bible studies and completed daily homework lessons. But in this time of crisis, Vicki explains she needed more.

Every day, throughout the day, Vicki read Scripture. She got up early to find God's message for her. She recorded the verses in her journal and reflected those verses back to God in prayer. She listened to Christian radio, and sometimes Bible verses would jump out at her from the message and the lyrics.

She underlined verses. Her Bible became dog-eared because she was desperate to know what to do. She needed God's strength in order to obey His will. She says, "God's Word came alive for me in a new way. I had studied it and even memorized it, but now there was intensity. It was as though a passage or a verse was there on the page to communicate something specific to me."

She says God told her to stay in the marriage—to stay prayerful and faithful and to believe Tony would repent and return to his faith.

It was a long, difficult separation but Tony finally came home, first to God, and then in February 2008, to his family. God used Christian friends, their pastor, a Christian counselor, a Christian alcohol rehab program, and other resources throughout the journey. But Vicki knows ultimately the marriage was restored because God spoke to her from His Word.

Today Tony is not only the husband Vicki longed to have, he is also a father and grandfather who points his children and their families to Christ. He is active in his church and mentors young men. He speaks freely of his past mistakes, his repentance, and the grace he received from his Savior and his family.

When we read the Scriptures with a passion to know God and to hear from Him, He will meet us there among the stories and the teaching. We will stand with the Israelites and see God's glory fill the temple. We will grieve with Nehemiah over the condition of Jerusalem. We will mourn over our sin and pray with David:

"Create in me a pure heart, O God, and renew a steadfast spirit within me. Do not cast me from your presence or take your Holy Spirit from me. Restore to me the joy of your salvation and grant me a willing spirit, to sustain me. Then I will teach transgressors your ways, so that sinners will turn back to you" (Ps.51:10–13).

We will be in the crowd when Jesus feeds the 5,000 and in the temple court when He values the widow's mite because she gave all she had. We will hear Christ refute the legalism of the Pharisees. We will walk the long road to Calvary and stand at the foot of the cross. Along with Mary, our hearts jump and our spirits soar when the resurrected Master calls our name.[2]

Read the Bible today and encounter the living God. He will take the most difficult circumstances of your life; and by His grace He will bring you through suffering to glory. He will teach you, lead you, and give you joy in trial and the wisdom you desire. Make sure what you hear and believe is the voice of God.

13 LEAN FORWARD:
Replace Fear with Faith

When Satan slithered into the Garden, fear came too. With no shortage of things to be anxious about, believers and non-believers alike suffer stress and face uncertainty. For many of us, the struggle with fear keeps us from responding to God's call in our lives. We live staid, predictable lives, never experiencing the joy that comes when we follow, serve, give, or go.

We have heard the admonitions. "Don't be afraid. Release your fear to God." We know what we should do but we struggle with the practical. Simply trying harder doesn't work. Pep talks yield temporary results, but when a new challenge or an old problem arises, we land right back where we started.

God doesn't tell us to do the impossible. Since the Fall, God has been working His plan to restore His relationship with man, offering those who respond to Him the beautiful guarantee of His eternal presence.

God put a dream in Abram's heart and gave him a promise of a son in his very old age. "Do not be afraid, Abram. I am your shield, your very great reward " (Gen. 15:1).

The Israelites were caught between an advancing army and a sea of water. Moses delivered God's instructions. "Do not be afraid. Stand firm and you will see the deliverance the Lord will bring you today" (Exod. 14:13a).

God's people had arrived, but taking the Promised Land would not be easy. Enemies threatened. Great battles loomed. "Have I not commanded you? Be strong and courageous. Do not be frightened, and do not be dismayed, for the Lord your God is with you wherever you go" (Josh.1: 9 ESV).

Gabriel reassured the perplexed young virgin. "Do not be afraid, Mary; you have found favor with God" (Luke 1:30).

The angel called to terrified shepherds, "Do not be afraid. I bring you good news that will cause great joy for all the people" (Luke 2:10).

Fear not. You will receive the promise. *Fear not.* The Lord will deliver. *Fear not.* God will be with you. *Fear not.* This is God's plan. *Fear not.* God has come to dwell with man, and you are witnesses to the miracle.

This is not a watered-down, clichéd response given when nothing more can be offered; rather, "Do not be afraid!" is the clarion call proclaimed to all those who live in relationship with God.

Seven years ago, Marsha and Allen Lindsey adopted a child named Mattea. The young girl came to the couple with unique challenges. At the age of five, she had been attacked by a pit bull, leaving her with significant facial injuries. Her biological parents struggled with drugs and alcohol, leaving little Mattea to care for her own needs as best she could. Ultimately, by the grace of God and the intervention of many good people, she ended up in the Lindsey home. At first, everyone believed she would be there for a short time while her biological father pulled his own life together.

Marsha remembers her daughter's pain.

"Mattea suffered more in her first six years of life than most of us will ever know in a lifetime. One day, I was outside working in the yard. Mattea came to find me. Even as a seven year old, she wanted me to understand the way she thought and felt."

"She looked at me and said, 'All I ever wanted was a mama and daddy to love me and take care of me.' "

"Of course, I was overwhelmed with emotion. I told her that sometimes parents loved their children but don't know how to care for them. I said, 'That's when other people step-in to help and show the love.' "

Marsha says Mattea thought for a moment and then lit up with understanding. She asked, "Does that mean you'll be my step-in Mama? Will you will love me and take care of me?"

That's exactly what happened. Marsha and Allen showered the child with love and provided the security she needed. Gradually, Mattea blossomed into a confident, loving, young woman who sounds just like Marsha when she talks.

At the age of fourteen, the child is undergoing a series of operations that will restore her features. Her internal transformation, however, has been in process from the first day she met her adoptive family. She looks forward to the future. Although unsure of her outward appearance, Mattea knows she will continue to grow and thrive because she is treasured for the person God made her to be.

Mattea could neither will herself to be confident nor try harder to be joyful. For the last seven years, this little girl has received the complete and total acceptance of two extraordinary adoptive parents, an extended family, and a church that cares and invests in her life. Love triumphed and fear vanished.

The antidote to fear is not to try harder or be braver. Fear is defeated when we experience the depth of our Heavenly Father's love.

"If anyone acknowledges that Jesus is the Son of God, God lives in them and they in God. And so we know and rely on the love God has for us. God is love. Whoever lives in love lives in God, and God in them. This is how love is made complete among us so that we will have confidence on the day of judgment: In this world we are like Jesus. There is no fear in love. But perfect love drives out fear, because fear has to do with punishment. The one who fears is not made perfect in love" (1 John 4: 15–18).

John wrote these verses to believers to assure them they could be confident in the final judgment. That same confidence extends to our daily lives. It begins when we respond to Jesus' invitation to come and follow Him. As we grow to understand the extent and significance of God's love, we realize there is no reason to worry—about eternity or about tomorrow. The more we understand how God cares for us the easier it becomes to abandon ourselves to Him. Love replaces fear and prompts us to willingly take risks in our daily lives as we choose to live by faith.

Our eternal home will be free from pain and suffering and doubt and fear. The perfection will be in heaven when we finally meet Him face to face. Until that time, He tells us we will find Him when we search for Him with all our hearts. The more we know Him the more we love Him. The more we love Him the less we fear.

Having faith does not mean we won't struggle with doubt; rather, faith is a confidence that God will act in the future to bring about what He has promised. When we follow God, even though we don't know where we are going, we demonstrate our faith in His goodness and His power. When we make decisions based on the teachings of His Word, instead of on what would be easy and safe, we are acting in faith. Faith is not only a mental assent to God's character, it is also doing the thing He requires because we know we can trust Him to act on our behalf. Faith in God isn't a feeling about God but rather the decision to obey His Word.

When we experience great love, it spills over into the lives of other people. Recently, Marsha and Mattea made a trip to the local grocery store. Several young children began to stare. The startled looks turned to whispers and giggles. Marsha recognized what was happening and quickly tried to steer her daughter away from their unkind comments.

Mattea Lindsey, daughter of Marsha and Allen Lindsey, and beloved child of God, had already heard the harsh words. Instead of dissolving in tears or anger, the young woman looked forward to her future and spoke with great confidence and even compassion.

"They don't understand, Mom. They don't know all I've been through and how I came to this place to be with you. One day I'll have a regular face, and then when I look like everybody else, I will find them and explain my story. They need to know how much God loves them, too."

14 LEAN FORWARD:
Share Your Story

Jeremy and Lindsey Lee attract friends with their out-going dispositions and straightforward communication style. They have been instrumental in growing their Sunday School class and continue to make important contributions to several ministries within the church. Recently, the young couple faced a serious problem. The issue burdened their hearts and clouded their vision.

"I wanted a baby," explained Lindsey. "When it didn't arrive on schedule, I grew angry with God."

Jeremy said the desire to have a child took over his and Lindsey's relationship. "Lindsey spent every waking minute thinking about a baby and wondering why we didn't have a baby. I began to feel like she had forgotten all about me. There was an emotional distance, and I felt abandoned."

For Jeremy, the loneliness could not have come at a more difficult time. "My business was struggling. I care for both my grandparents and neither of them was doing very well. My mother's cancer had reoccurred. And now the most important relationship in my life was strained because we could not have a child."

Jeremy remembered when he reached a breaking point. "I saw all these people who were living any way they wanted and their lives looked just fine. Their businesses were successful. Their family was healthy. They had kids. I couldn't figure out what we were doing wrong."

One afternoon Jeremy stormed outside and looked up to pray. To anyone listening the words might have sounded more like a rant. Jeremy said he cried out, "God, I have prayed about all these things. I go to church. I tithe and read the Bible. I'm not asking you to fix everything. It would be great if just one thing worked, but right now I feel as if I can't catch a break."

It wasn't immediate, but Jeremy began to feel a supernatural kind of peace.

"God began to teach me about His faithfulness. It's like He was saying, 'I've got this, Jeremy. You don't have to worry about me taking care of you. Your job is to have a testimony that can reach other people.'"

Lindsey told a similar story. "For awhile I lived in my anger. Then I began to meet with a Christian friend on a weekly basis. She understood me because she had been through a similar experience. She encouraged me to be honest with God. When I spent time really talking to God, expressing my feelings to Him, my perspective began to change."

Lindsey said she thought about how much God loved her and the gifts He had given. Her gratitude lifted her spirits. She realized how she had harbored her angry feelings. The young woman confessed first to God and then to her husband.

God showed Lindsey she was not the only one who had ever struggled with infertility. She said, "I had to choose to believe God would work in my situation to bring something good to pass. It took prayer and some time, but gradually I got to the point where I could say that life would be good even if I didn't have a baby. I wanted what God wanted."

When Lindsey and Jeremy were honest with God, they also became honest with each other and worked through the stress in their own relationship. The couple resolved to wait on God's timing.

Jeremy explained, "I realized that always, in every situation, God had taken care of us. Many times it is in ways I do not expect. He has taught us to live by faith."

The circumstances had not changed, but the darkness had gone. Lindsey and Jeremy traveled from anger to acceptance, determined to live with a testimony of God's grace proclaimed from their lips and revealed in their lives.

Soon Lindsey felt God's gentle nudge toward adoption, something she had been reluctant to consider. Jeremy wasn't interested.

"I shot her down when she talked about adoption. I told her God would talk to both of us if He wanted us to adopt."

Jeremy admitted he wasn't prepared for what happened next.

"Five nights in a row, I dreamed about adoption. I didn't mention it to Lindsey at all because I didn't want her to know I was struggling again. I had no peace. On the sixth morning I got up and sat in my chair and told God I was ready and willing to adopt, if that was what He was calling us to do."

Jeremy said one of his greatest concerns involved finances. He understood the expense. He knew when they began the process they would need to have $10,000 almost immediately and another $20,000 available in a year's time.

The young man determined to take a third job and begin to save his earnings. He thought when they had fifteen thousand saved he would tell Lindsey they could begin the paperwork.

Lindsey wanted to begin the process immediately—even without the savings on hand. "I just knew that if God wanted us to adopt that He would provide the money. I appreciated and respected my husband immensely for being financially smart and prudent. But at the same time, I wanted him to just take a leap of faith with me. Jeremy tried to keep me grounded by reminding me of the amount he wanted to save and how long it would probably take to get that much. I felt like it would be a year or longer before we could start our paperwork. I kept joking and saying that I wish some money would just fall out of the sky."

God answered the couple's prayers in an amazing way.

Lindsey explained, "Several families gave us the cash we needed to begin the adoption process. We are still shocked but so incredibly grateful that there are people who have such giving hearts."

For eighteen months the Lee's lived through interviews and paperwork, red tape and security clearances. Eventually, they received a photo of their daughter and more information about her medical condition and background.

This past summer, Jeremy and Lindsey traveled to China, where they finalized the adoption of their little girl. Ella Blair is beautiful, happy, and the delight of her parents' lives.

Lindsey blogged about the adoption journey, sharing the heartache, the fear, and the joy they've experienced along the way.

The couple said the waiting was not easy. Throughout the adoption process, they chose to focus on God's goodness and plan for their lives. Lindsey prays God will use their story in several ways.

The Lees want other people to be drawn to Christ so that He receives the glory. Lindsey believes she will be able to help other people who travel a similar road.

She has come to a new conclusion. "So many times you hear that God doesn't give you more than you can handle. I'm not sure that statement is anywhere in the Bible. I believe that God does give you more than you can handle, so that the only thing you can do is cling to Him. If we could do this on our own, we would never have a need for God."

When Lindsey and Jeremy look back on the last seven years of their marriage, they can see how they have changed and grown. Their pain pushed them deeper into the heart of God. He was faithful and gave the strength they needed, one day at a time.

Lindsey doesn't dwell on the "whys" any longer. The questions have changed to "how?" and "what?" How does God want me to walk through this time of life? What can I do to bring others to Him? What can I do to bring Him glory?

The young woman knows for certain that you can't take people to a place you've never been. Lindsey prays for others and uses her story to encourage others who are going through a similar situation.

"We could have lost this chance to influence people for Christ. If we seemed angry and unapproachable, no one would ever listen to what we have to say." The Lees are discovering what many others already know. There is great joy in allowing God to turn trouble into triumph. Something exciting occurs when we turn around and share our experience with another person.

When I began publishing a Christian magazine I knew I wanted to inspire believers to love God more deeply and follow Christ with passion and purpose. I wanted to connect the Christian community, focusing on what we have in common rather than the less significant issues that keep us from working and praying together. I wanted to highlight mission and ministry opportunities and encourage people to put feet to their faith.

I discovered the way to accomplish the vision was actually pretty simple. We inspired, connected, and motivated believers by telling their stories. Men and women, teens and teachers, doctors and store clerks spoke about their faith in Jesus and their journey to knowing Him. Our readers could relate to the pain, the decisions, and the grace and guidance of God.

Scripture speaks frequently about the role of each generation. Charged with an awesome responsibility, we are to transfer our faith to the people coming behind us—to our sons, our daughters, and our grandchildren. We are to tell co-workers and the neighbors what God has done in our lives.

People are most receptive to our faith when our words sound authentic. Although we might prefer to look perfectly pulled together, people are most interested in what happens when they know we are struggling too.

Our pain becomes meaningful when we realize at some point God will connect us with people who need the love and wisdom we have to offer. We will put what we have experienced to use, for the benefit of others and the glory of God.

"All praise to God, the Father of our Lord Jesus Christ. God is our merciful Father and the source of all comfort. He comforts us in all our troubles so that we can comfort others. When they are troubled, we will be able to give them the same comfort God has given us" (2 Corinthians 1:3-4, NLT).

You have something to say. Your experiences have taught you about God's mercy and grace. You have a message others need to know. Don't linger in the past. Allow your difficulties to become a part of the narrative of your life. Reflect on your struggles in the light of God's grace. Think and speak of your pain in the light of redemption. When you open your life to another person you will encourage them in their walk. You will also find meaning in your own pain as you listen to God, discern how you should respond, and plan what you will do.

15 LEAN FORWARD:
Desire the Change

But grow in the grace and knowledge of our Lord and Savior
Jesus Christ. To him be glory both now and forever! Amen.
— *2 Peter 3:18*

The routines of life can keep us from transformation or lead us straight to the heart of God. Good intentions don't really matter. The practices outlined in this book are not going to slip into your life in an unexpected way. You won't wake up one morning and suddenly realize you've developed the habit of prayer. You won't suddenly discover you have become grateful or forgiving. Another's story will encourage and inspire, but you must make the decision and do the work.

You must want spiritual transformation. You must want to hear from God and be willing to cooperate with the process.

The movement through any of these disciplines is a movement toward God. It is a movement toward relationship and wisdom. You won't make the sacrifices unless you believe in the worth of the objective.

The outcome exceeds the effort. We begin to think and respond like Jesus because God blesses our offerings. The Spirit takes the Word of God, our kingdom prayers, and our receptive hearts to transform our lives. When we cooperate with the Spirit, we position ourselves to hear from God.

We want instant gratification; however, that's not the way God works. Dallas Willard says it this way. "God is not going to pick us up by the seat of our pants, as it were, and throw us into transformed kingdom living, into 'holiness.'" [1]

In 2011, when I discovered we would be moving, I responded in my typical fashion. At first I fumed and fussed and worried. I wanted to predict the future. Eventually, I realized my words, feelings, and attempts at control weren't going to change the circumstances; but they were certainly making me miserable.

I had already spent hours praying about the situation when I felt a prompting of the Spirit.

Write down what you already know you are supposed to do.

This time I listened and obeyed. I sat down and made this list:

- *Memorize Scripture for direction and wisdom.*
- *Prepare in advance.*
- *Change my perspective.*
- *Get rid of distractions.*
- *Confess my part in any problem.*
- *Forgive those who have harmed me.*
- *Practice gratitude.*
- *Do the next thing.*
- *Connect with other believers.*
- *Pray with the kingdom in mind.*
- *Replace Satan's lies with God's truth.*
- *Replace fear with faith.*
- *Tell my story.*

I recognized I would not be able to do any of these things on my own. I also knew the value would be lost if this list became a legalistic way of living.

Any movement toward God happens because of the grace of God. The Spirit stirs us and gives us both the desire and the ability to obey. The person who grows to be most like Jesus isn't someone who runs around and attempts to do more and more on their own. A transformed person allows God's grace to consume them and overflow into every aspect of their life.

Today, my chair sits on the second floor of our new home. I'm tucked into an alcove with a window overlooking our back yard. It's almost like I'm in a tree house—the best kind of tree house—comfortable, air-conditioned, and bug-free.

My surroundings are quiet and my soul is too.

Jim and I believe God guided us to this community at this time for specific purposes. Our lives are to be lived in a way that bring glory to God and advance His kingdom.

When the door opened wide for us in Albany, Georgia, I wondered aloud what I would do with myself in this new community. Without hesitation my husband said, "Write a book."

Although the idea was intimidating, I agreed this could be where God was taking me. I tried to get started right away, but we were waiting to finalize our plans and there were too many distractions. I prayed over the idea and began to think about what God might want to say through me—if I ever could muster the concentration and sit in one place long enough.

I spent one month unpacking and getting settled in our new community. Then, when most of the boxes were empty, I knew it was time to begin.

What I have presented in these pages is not a list of rules you must follow to get to heaven. Jesus paid the price for your salvation on the cross. Because of Jesus, you live in relationship with the holy God. There is nothing you can do to make God love you any more or any less.

He knew you even before you were born. He made you, not so He would have a distant subject to order around and control, but so He would have a child He could love and shower with goodness. He loved you enough to send Jesus to take the penalty you deserved. The cross is proof of God's love. It's a perfect love that always acts in your best interest.

God has been with me every step of every journey I have taken. I have felt His presence in this transition as much or more than at any time in my life. I have discovered it is possible to walk through difficult situations with a love for God and the knowledge that He will direct my path.

This confidence in God doesn't mean I don't have questions or the occasional restless feeling. I long for connections, and those deep relationships don't form quickly. I am waiting to belong. But as I wait, I lean forward in an effort to hear God's voice. I don't want to miss any opportunity, any relationship, any change and development He wants me to experience. Thankfully, I have learned that God doesn't waste anything, even in the days of waiting. God speaks in every situation.

When I began to write about the things God has taught me, I quickly realized how intertwined they are. You can't really separate forgiveness from prayer. Your gratitude increases when you live in community with other believers. You replace Satan's lies with God's truth, and you realize your need to confess your own sins.

Even though these disciplines are woven together, God has brought them to my attention separately. I think He wants me to identify and name them specifically, enabling me to improve and grow in each area without feeling overwhelmed. So today, He may remind me to memorize His Word. Tomorrow the passage or verse that I memorized will encourage me to forgive someone who may have hurt my feelings, whether purposefully or through neglect.

These disciplines are not legalistic exercises but they give me a framework in which growth can occur.

As a little girl, I filled out offering envelopes on Saturday night. The outside of the envelope included a place to record our weekly faithfulness. I thought of it as earning points. I got a point for reading my Bible each day. I got a point for giving money. I got a point for bringing a friend to church. The point system, however, will not sustain motivation and sometimes makes us fudge the facts.

You don't earn access to God by checking boxes. Hearing from Him is about making room in your life for the relationship. This relationship is not a static thing. The more I know Him, the more I realize how much more I want of Him. The more I understand the difference He makes in my life, the more I look for Him in every situation. I orient my thoughts and my time in this way. He has promised to reveal Himself to me when I search for Him with all my heart.

"When you come looking for me, you'll find me. Yes, when you get serious about finding me and want it more than anything else, I'll make sure you won't be disappointed." (Jeremiah 29:13, MSG).

When we position ourselves to hear God's voice, a transformation takes place inside our hearts and minds. We are different in the way we think and the way we feel, and that translates into how we look to other people.

The time we spend drawing near to God is not meant to make us strange so that we repel those who don't know Jesus. The disciplines transform the way we think and see our situations. We live more confidently, and that confidence is attractive to the world.

When I was younger, I thought about life as a series of chapters. When I had kids or my kids went to school, or when Jim and I had more time together, or when I figured out my mission in life, I would reach the happily ever after part of the book. Today I understand the restlessness I sometimes feel is not really related to my circumstances. It's a part of my life because I am a believer and I am not home.

Heaven is my ultimate destination. Heaven is where my questions will be answered and my relationships will be perfect. Heaven is where the barriers will be removed and I will finally become the person God created me to be.

One day all believers will see God face to face. We won't be encumbered by sin that chokes the beauty from our world. No longer will we be limited by our own understanding or past experiences.

The apostle Paul said it like this: "We don't yet see things clearly. We're squinting in a fog, peering through a mist. But it won't be long before the weather clears and the sun shines bright! We'll see it all then, see it all as clearly as God sees us, knowing him directly just as he knows us!" (1 Cor.13:12, MSG).

In eternity, we will know Him even as He knows us now. Our love for Him will be complete and perfect as His love for us has always been. Heaven is our beautiful, glorious future where there will be no more suffering, no more strained relationships, and no more sleepless nights filled with worry and pain. We will live in perfect relationship with God and with those who also gave their lives to love and serve the Lord Jesus Christ.

Until we see Him face to face, we must listen carefully, look closely, and faithfully follow where He leads.

He who has ears, let him hear. Jesus frequently told his followers to listen. (This expression is recorded at least six times in the Gospel accounts of Jesus' ministry.[2])

He urged them to remove all obstacles that prevented them from focusing their attention on what God was saying.

We live an incredible life in relationship with the God of the universe who speaks and leads us throughout each day. As we hear Him speak to us, we open the door to our transformation. Our thoughts and feelings begin to reflect the principles of Scripture. We find ourselves responding to people and situations like Jesus would respond.

The transformation process is the road to knowing God. And when we know God, we know what to do.

God's work in our lives is always for our good and His glory—there is no hidden agenda with Him. He promises to meet our needs when we invest ourselves in a relationship with Him. In times of pain, doubt, and indecision God wants to wrap you in His arms and hold you close. He stands ready to pour life and love into the depth of your soul.

Lean forward, today. Position yourself to hear Him speak.

Notes

Chapter 2
[1]Richard Foster, Celebration of Discipline (New York: Harper Collins, 1998), 19
[2]Psalm 103:1–5
[3]Dallas Willard, Hearing God (Downers Grove, IL: IVP Books, 1999), 18

Chapter 3
[1] Dallas Willard, Renovation of the Heart (Colorado Springs: NavPress, 2002), 14

Chapter 4
[1] Timothy Keller, King's Cross (New York, Dutton, 2011), 30
[2] Andrew Murray, Waiting on God, Returning to the Place of Absolute Dependence (Fort Washington, PA: CLC Publications, 1999), 121
[3]Mark 6:45-52
[4]Philip Yancey, Reaching for the Invisible God, (Grand Rapids: Zondervan, 2000), 261
[5]Larry Crabb, Connecting (Nashville: Thomas Nelson, 1997), 111

Chapter 5
[1] Put Down the Duckie, Music by Christopher Cerf, Lyrics by Norman Stiles, 1986
[2] Joan Gale Thomas, If Jesus Came To My House (New York: HarperCollins, 1951)
[3]Dallas Willard, Hearing God (Downers Grove, IL: IVP Books, 1999), 91

Chapter 6
[1] Richard Foster, Celebration of Discipline (New York: HarperCollins, 1998) 157

Notes Continued

Chapter 7

[1] Genesis 3:1b

[2] Genesis 3: 4

[3] Brian Jones, Getting Rid of The Gorilla. Confessions on the Struggle to Forgive (Cincinnati, Ohio: Standard Publishing, 2008), 27

[4] Gordon McDonald, A Resilient Life (Nashville, Thomas Nelson, 2004), 129

Chapter 8

[1] Romans 12:12

[2] Luke 17:11–19

[3] Mark 10:46–52

Chapter 9

[1] Dallas Willard, Renovation of the Heart (Colorado Springs: NavPress, 2002), 154

[2] Francis Chan, The Forgotten God, (Colorado Springs: David C. Cook, 2009) 120

[3] Elisabeth Eliott, backtothebible.org. Gateway to Joy, Do the Next Thing

Chapter 10

[1] James 1:19–21; 2:3–4

[2] Dietrich Bonhoeffer, Life Together (New York: HarperCollins, 1954), 30

Chapter 11

[1] John 17

[2] Matthew 26:36–44; Mark 14:36–42; Luke 22:39–42

[3] Dallas Willard, Hearing God (Downers Grove, IL: IVP Books, 1999), 91

Notes Continued

Chapter 12

[1]Matthew 3:13–4:11; Luke 3:21–22; 4:1–13

[2]John 20:11-18

Chapter 15

[1]Dallas Willard, Renovation of the Heart, (Colorado Springs; NavPress, 2002), 91

[2]Matthew 11:15; 13:9, 43; Mark 4:9; Luke 8:8, 14:35

26050208R00069

Made in the USA
Charleston, SC
22 January 2014